The Hummingbird Kiss:

My Life as an Addict in the 1970s

by **Trish MacEnulty**

ISBN 979-8-9876450-5-5

Published by
Prism Light Press
info@prismlightpress.com

Manufactured in the United States of America.

First edition published 2021 by Prism Light Press

In memory of my mother, Rosalind,
who never once stopped believing in me
and for my brothers, John and David

PRAISE FOR TRISH MACENULTY'S WRITING

A frank, moving depiction of a nightmarish slice of American life.

—*Kirkus Reviews*

An immensely energetic story of a drug addict and all that implies. Alternately harrowing, funny and heartbreaking, the book showcases MacEnulty's talent for producing a strong narrative drive, as well as for delivering a perceptive, lively and decidedly unsentimental version of what could have easily been a seedy, exploitive tale in the hands of a less gifted writer.

—*Creative Loafing*

It is entirely to MacEnulty's credit that she confronts her demons head-on in a hilarious, unflinching vital account devoid of sentiment or platitude.

—*The Glasgow Herald*

MacEnulty writes about her subject with sympathy, wisdom and - an unexpected blessing - humour. . . We are spared no detail of her sordid descent, but Trish remains an engaging character whose innate, if often subdued, grain of goodness and interest in humanity keeps the reader on her side. Against the odds, Trish declines to blame anyone for her calamitous state.

— *The Guardian Unlimited*

MacEnulty has constructed a gritty and sorrowful book about a young girl with an appetite for the damage done....Trish's take on the world is tragic and rueful, and not once does she glorify the tough life she has chosen for herself.

— *The San Diego Union - Tribune*

MacEnulty meticulously develops the story of people on the edge fighting to regain a foothold to life. Without sentimentality or pop psychology, the author richly explores what led Trish to drugs... a tough, uncompromising story that at the same time hinges on the belief that people can change their lives.

— *South Florida Sun-Sentinel*

Contents

Foreword

This is a true story, but it's not always factual. I actually have two brothers. I melded them into one. Several other characters are also composites. All the names except my own have been changed. But those are surface details. I have omitted or altered some episodes for the sake of brevity and privacy. Otherwise, this is the life I led, the life I left behind. At least, this is what I remember. Those who might quibble with me over the details, they're dead.

A version of this story was originally published by Serpent's Tail Press as a novel called *Sweet Fire*.

Take Me to the River

Thin yellow light crept through the crack in the curtains, as Al Green sang "Take me to the River" on my clock radio. It was seven o'clock. I rolled out of bed and padded into the bathroom for a quick shower.

My new husband, Charlie, was under court order to stay with his parents until his sentencing, which was that morning in a half an hour. I figured it was my duty to show up, but I did not want to go. My mind felt gummy, I kept sneezing, my back ached, and for some reason I couldn't stop yawning. What a day to be getting a cold.

I flung back the blue shower curtain and turned on the hot water. Everything in my mother's bathroom was blue: the throw rug, the towels, the cover over the back of the toilet seat. A blue nude, painted by one of my mom's artist friends, hung on the wall. Charlie had been fascinated. His parents were Mormons and they didn't own paintings, especially blue nudes.

"Your mother is like someone from another planet," he said, which is how Charlie himself felt around his family. What my mother said about Charlie is another story, especially after the time he pawned her mink coat and denied it up to the last gasping second when she dropped the pawn ticket on the table.

I stood in the shower with the water running over me. My skin felt raw, and the water fell on me like mercury. I washed my hair, breathing in the heady scent of Herbal Essence, as Charlie's day in court played itself like a bad television show in my head. Since the old learned judge was a friend of Charlie's family, he'd probably get more probation or maybe they'd send him back to that lame-ass drug program.

Charlie and I had managed to inject a bit of dope every day for at least a month. My veins could use a break. I rinsed, turned off the water and stepped out of the tub. The drain swallowed the last dregs of lathery water. I sneezed again.

My mother was still in bed. I didn't wake her. She would have felt obligated to get up, make breakfast or something. I wasn't hungry, and I didn't want to exchange pleasantries. Isn't this a glorious day to watch your incorrigible husband get spanked in public?

I trotted downstairs to the kitchen of our apartment, which was clean and shining and quiet as a chapel with the soft gray light streaming through the oak trees into the window. I boiled some water in a white tea kettle and made a cup of Orange Pekoe tea, but at the first sip, I had to run to the sink and vomit. Not the sweet effortless regurgitation brought on by a robust shot of warm heroin, but a gagging bile-filled puke.

A cold and a stomach flu. For God's sake, I thought. I tossed the tea into the sink, rinsed out my mouth and grabbed my purse. I stopped by the mirror to smear on some lipstick and was caught by the black holes inside my green irises—cat eyes, Charlie called them. I stood there for a moment in front of the gold-framed mirror like a portrait of myself: my long dark hair and the blond streaks I'd recently added out of boredom, framing my pale oval face. Something about my eyes looked just like Charlie did that time he told me he was dope sick and needed to pawn my watch for a fix. I dropped my leather purse, swallowed and leaned toward my reflection.

I had it. The jones. That's what they called it. Charlie and his friends. The jones or the bear. I examined the pastiness of my skin and noticed the sniffling and the way my back ached. Well, what else had I expected? All this time, I'd never let him get high without me because it wasn't fair. Not I--the chump who bakes cookies at home and waits for her man to come back all stoned and feeling good. Now, everything had changed—in the blink of my weirdly dilated eyes. A chill clawed its way down my back like little rats' feet.

I slipped on a jacket and stepped out of my mom's apartment into the empty embrace of the morning. Down past the end of the parking lot, the bare hands of the wind ruffled the river. A shower of brown oak leaves dropped onto the asphalt. But nothing felt normal.

I got into my Mazda, cranked the engine, turned on the radio and drove away, heading to the toll bridge where I tossed a quarter into the gaping mouth of the automatic toll booth. I watched the silver disk swirl around and around before plunking down the throat of the machine. The light turned green, and I flew across the river, swerving between pokey drivers who didn't really want to get to their awful jobs, and squinting my eyes against the sharp crackle of the sun's rays as it made its ascent—as if this were just another day. Until finally, I jettisoned out of my car, hurried through the heavy glass doors of the courthouse, darted into the elevator, and strode into the courtroom where in front of the judge's bench stood my lean and handsome husband, impersonating a young man with a future.

Goodtime Charlie

I found a seat next to my mother-in-law. Charlie's dad wasn't there, which seemed odd, but all I could think about was getting out of there and finding a little piece of oblivion. I wore Charlie's favorite perfume, Chanel No. 9, and a red pinstriped dress with a belted waist. My fingers knotted themselves nervously.

Charlie stood with his back to us, facing the judge. His hair gleamed, the glossy color of cockroach wings, just above the collar of his Oxford shirt. His hands dangled at his sides, and he shifted his weight from one foot to the other. His baldheaded lawyer leaned in toward the judge.

Charlie's mother sat motionless next to me, her thin lips pressed tight against her teeth. She barely breathed. As soon as Charlie got his probation reinstated, he and I would go cop. Then my nose would stop leaking and the ache in my back would ease. Even if he got sent back to the drug program, they'd give him a day to get his things ready.

It was my first time in a court of law. I was 18. I looked around, waiting for something to happen. The courtroom was impressive, modern and cavernous. Those high paneled walls and the beamed ceiling made me feel like a flea. The old judge stared down at his files showing only the gray top of his head while Charlie's expensive lawyer spoke to him in low tones as if he were selling a used car to the judge, trying to convince him of the car's road-worthiness, trying to distract him from the fact there was no transmission under the hood.

When the lawyer stopped talking, the judge lifted his head as if from prayer and gazed at Charlie. Charlie sniffled. He had it, too, I thought. He'd gotten clean in the drug program but these past few weeks he'd made up for lost time. The judge stared into the black pits of Charlie's eyes. Then he said in a gentle, grandfatherly voice, "I sentence you to ten years in the state penitentiary."

Charlie's mother did not make a sound, but her chin dropped, and she looked as if the blood had instantaneously disappeared from her body. She reminded me of a translucent cicada shell like the ones I'd find in my yard as a kid. Charlie's head snapped around, and his wide, terrified eyes locked on to his mama. His pale skin grew even paler, his gaunt face even gaunter. I wanted to shake myself awake. Ten years? All he did was steal some lousy stereos and then skip out on the court-ordered drug program. But by the expression on Charlie's face--the quivering lips, the heavy-lidded eyes round as saucers--I knew that I hadn't heard wrong.

Charlie's mom clutched her purse and stood up. She took one more look at her son, her darling boy, and he looked back at her, his eyes wet and shining. Then she left the courtroom. I stayed and watched as the bailiff led Charlie through a doorway and out of our lives. Our eyes met just before the door closed. I stared at his face, thick eyebrows, crooked nose, sharp chin. Then the door shut.

Outside the courtroom Charlie's mother and I waited for the interminable elevator. She wiped a tear away quickly and said in her choked southern drawl, "I can't believe it. What will I tell his father?"

I stared down at the leather Aigner pumps on my feet. I didn't know what to say to her. I was stunned. I thought about Charlie's milky pale skin, the tufts of hair around his nipples, the way he smelled like rainwater. What would I do with myself now that he was gone? What about right now? My nose was running like a faucet. My spine twisted in its shell. Charlie was supposed to be free, and right now we should have been our way to cop some dope.

The elevator doors opened like curtains to the next act and there stood Charlie's younger brother—the good boy.

"Is it over already?" he asked.

Charlie's mom didn't answer. She just sobbed as he took her in his arms while I pushed the L button.

"He got ten years," I said. Charlie's brother patted his mother on the back. He was not as surprised as we were.

I rode down with them to the lobby, walked past the blind lady selling gum and went outside to the parking lot. Charlie's mom had never been particularly fond of me, but she invited me over to the house.

"No, thank you," I told her as if she'd asked me over for sherry and a cheese ball with crackers, as if I were deeply sorry but simply had too many pressing engagements. My mother would have been proud of my manners. But I just didn't want to deal with his family.

Charlie and I had only been married three months—by the second month he'd been sentenced to the drug program for the stolen stereo, then we spent two weeks on the run and the last two weeks back at our parents' respective abodes after Charlie had gotten picked up by the cops. Even then we'd met during the day for our jaunts downtown to find dope and then lie around someone's crib watching soap operas. I felt bad for him, but I felt even worse for myself. It wasn't supposed to be like this—me alone today with dope-starved termites gnawing in my brain.

I watched as the two of them got in her Lincoln and drove off. In charge of large claims at the biggest life insurance company in town, she had never missed a day of work until today. I felt sad and didn't like it.

I walked along the waterfront toward my car. The river, brown and wide, kept pace with me, like a stray dog that joins you on a walk. It had that familiar smell of dead fish and oil. Renegade water. It smelled like my life. Just down the street was Billy's Pawn and Gun Shop where Charlie and I had taken our wedding rings two days earlier. And two blocks east of that was the building where Charlie's mom worked and where I had worked in the mailroom during the summer and where Charlie had waited for me outside every day and taken me to lunch at the Soul Food Cafe on Ashley Street. Another block down from that was Lucky's Lounge and Package Store, a scandalous place with fights bursting through the doors, dudes packing guns in their waistbands and women carrying switchblades, and where some master of enterprise always had a few bags of dope to sell in the parking lot.

Although it was wintertime, the weather was warm. I shed my jacket, closed my eyes, and turned my face up toward the burning light of the sun. A cold dagger traveled from my skull to a sharp point between my legs. I opened my eyes and gazed down at the roughed-up surface of the water.

Thoughts came to me from the bottom of my belly. I was a married woman, but I had no man. I had wanted to be married, thought it might make a difference, thought I would be okay if someone wanted me. But Charlie never wanted me more than he wanted a bag of dope. And me, what had I wanted out of it? I still wasn't sure. I wanted to be the kind of girl someone could love. And I wanted to be like ordinary people, people who got married and had cookouts with their friends, but that was like saying I wanted to raise my arms and fly. Fat chance. And now I had a dope habit.

A seagull swooped over the water, gathered speed, and kept going. I watched until it disappeared. Then it hit me: Charlie had already taught me everything I needed to know. I didn't need him. I had some money in my wallet, and I knew where he always went to cop. Why not go by myself? I didn't even glance back at the jail standing tall and windowless like a giant mausoleum where Charlie was now facing a very different life.

I got in my car. The warm vinyl smell inside reminded me of those blistery summer days with Charlie, driving with no particular place to go. The only responsibility we faced was an obligation to get high, but it hadn't been a need for me, just an adventure, a chance to live the boys' life, which seemed exciting, filled with laughter and adrenaline — Huck Finn with the added element of self-destruction. But now I felt an edginess. Shooting heroin was not just a social activity. It had a call, and I could hear it for the first time like a child recognizing its mother's voice.

I rolled down the window and let a gentle January breeze blow across my face as I drove through the city. Jacksonville was a big sweat-stained town. It existed in my mind as if it were in a book, the sun falling down the shabby streets, everything a little old and disreputable, a little rundown. A city in patchy overalls. The streets felt forlorn. Originally it was called Cowford, then the Civil War came, next the yellow fever and after that a fire from a cigar factory swept through the streets. A different kind of fever possessed the place now, and a quiet, unquenchable fire.

Charlie used to say, "The people in this town have larceny in their hearts, Baby. Larceny."

Well, he should know. I would miss his swamp-water voice, low and southern. His voice could wrap its arms around me and soothe my wild temper. I loved his voice more than anything else about him. Of course, it was different when he had with his cronies with him, and they were laughing, and quoting some Rudy Ray Moore record. I felt like I was observing a secret club.

"I'm Petey Wheatstraw, the devil's son-in-law and the high sheriff of hell," Charlie would say, with a whine when he said "high" as if it were an incantation. He'd laugh and continue, "I sandpapered an elephant's asshole to fit this big dick." As if Charlie had any use for a dick besides taking a piss. He had stopped even pretending to care about sex.

As I reached the city blocks where the Black people stood outside with watchful eyes and laughing mouths, I downshifted, my muscles loosening their grip on my bones. I felt more comfortable in this part of town. There was a life and liveliness that was missing from the staid old white parts of the city. People didn't lock themselves away and throw false smiles at each other from their windows.

I saw our connection, Gentleman Jim, and pulled over. He bent down and looked at me through the passenger window like a preacher, carrying the gospel. I leaned over and rolled down the window.

"Where's your old man, Baby?" he asked. Charlie always called me baby, and so that had become my moniker in these circles.

"He just got a dime," I said, aware that I had shocking news and now I had to someone to share it with.

"Ten years? Damn," he said, hands in pockets, looking down at the ground and shaking his head. "Damn." Then, "You want to cop?"

I nodded. Step One.

"How much?"

"A trés," I said. Why we junkies spoke in French, I never knew.

"Okay," he said. Two for me. One for him for copping. He slid into the car with me, and I drove around the corner. I handed over 25 dollars, Step Two; he got out and slipped into a bar, Step Three. Gentleman Jim was generally pretty slow, but today he came back quickly and gave me my two tinfoil bags. Two bags all to myself. Charlie usually short-changed me, giving me little g-shots while he got good and greasy. No one would ever give me a g-shot again. After promising to come back soon, I drove off. Everything seemed inevitable and easy, weirdly easy. How to cop dope in three easy steps.

Upstairs in the bathroom of my mom's townhouse, I took out my works, my bottle cap, the knee-high hose I used for a tie and my matches. Mom wasn't home but even if she was, I didn't care. I was thinking of my independence. I could cop by myself, I could get off by myself, I even knew how to jimmy open a locked door with a screwdriver. Not only did I not need Charlie anymore. I didn't need anybody. These were my thoughts as I poked through my skin and into the vein inside my elbow, saw the blood announce entrance like a waving flag and then pushed the plunger down.

As I did so, a warm prickling kiss swept from my nose, up over my eyes, down my neck, along my back, lingering moistly in every part of my body until it settled in my knees. Just like that, I had stepped through the curtains and I stood on another stage in a murky, phantasmagoric reality. Heroin was the key to a dream world. You just had to know how to make it work. And now I did.

Moon River

My mother was 37 when she gave birth to me in a hospital overlooking the St. John's River. All the hospitals in Jacksonville hunkered down next to the river, a convenient place to dump waste. My brother drove my mother to the hospital though he was only thirteen. My father was on a bender while, under the sign of Sagittarius with a moon in Pisces, a shrieking me was dragged by a pair of forceps into the world from my mother's twilight sleeping body.

"I felt like I was in a prison in that marriage," my mother once told me.

"Why did you marry him?" I wanted to know.

"I fell in love with his mind," she replied. "I didn't know he'd become an alcoholic." Her own father, a renowned judge who had left his wife and four kids in the middle of the depression, was also an alcoholic. She might have ditched my father long before she did if alcoholism hadn't had such a familiar feel to it.

Sometimes I wonder whether her feelings of imprisonment were imprinted onto me even as a fetus. As if the script of my life had been inscribed onto my DNA.

When I am three years old, I live with my mom, a black dog, and a big boy who keeps snakes. Sometimes the boy rages like a lunatic, but he is not mad at me. When I sit beside him, I can feel the anger blow off him in waves. But he never raises his voice to me. My mother plays the piano, and her face gets sad, and she flies away from us. I like to pretend I am a cat named Spotty and crawl across the dark linoleum kitchen floor. I make a nest of blankets under the long wooden table. Sometimes at night a man comes into this house. Everything gets loud then. I don't know what I've done. I hide when he comes. I hide under my bed, in my closet, anywhere I can. Once I ran out into the woods behind our house and my brother had to come out and find me. But no matter what I do, I cannot get away from that yelling, booming, angry voice. Did I see my mother fall like a tall pine tree? Or did I dream it as a picture-book illustration to the yelling, booming angry voice?

See, my mother says, when I am older and the man never comes anymore, this is your daddy holding you. See how much he loves you.

I look at the picture. Yes, the man with the black-night voice smiles and the little baby smiles back.

But my father never took to his children. As we grew up, we tried to connect with him, but he always wanted to fight my brother and he had no idea what to say to me. He never gave us presents or took us anywhere. Once on Father's Day, when I was in my 20s, I took him out to lunch. He said something to the effect of "Mothers can't help but love their children, but a father's love must be earned."

So that's it, I thought. I hadn't "earned" his love. Silly me.

Midnight Special

After Charlie got the rude awakening of a lifetime, I had to get the hell out of Dodge. I couldn't let heroin rule my life, not like I'd seen it rule his. For one thing, I didn't have the money. For another, the thought of spending ten years in prison for the love of dope made me want to take an axe to my brain. I felt about as lonely as one of those experimental monkey babies taken from its mother, clutching onto a wire mother, its face the definition of despair.

I came downstairs the morning after the sentencing. I'd cleaned out the residue in the cooker and was reasonably comfortable. My mom sat at the table, eating her breakfast toast with orange marmalade, the newspaper spread before her. She stopped chewing and looked up at me with something like sympathy. I sat down and stared at the sports section.

"Hungry?" she asked.

I shook my head. She probably thought I was grieving. If she thought anything else, she didn't say.

"It's a shame," she said. No matter what she thought of Charlie, she didn't like to see anyone get locked up, especially a boy only twenty-one years old.

"Mom, I need to get away for a while," I told her. I didn't tell her why, and she didn't ask. There were things she didn't want to know.

"Where do you want to go?" she asked.

"I thought I'd go visit Shannon," I said. Shannon had been my best friend since seventh grade. We hadn't seen much of each other the last couple of years especially since she went off to college and I didn't. Which was a big sore point with my mom. I was the one who'd made straight A's even while I was the reigning queen of the high school dopers. Shannon was lucky to have a C average. But her parents had buckets full of money, and Shannon hadn't decided to fall in love with and marry a dope addict.

"I think that's a good idea," my mother said.

I made a couple of phone calls, packed a suitcase and that afternoon I had a coach seat on a plane to Philadelphia. The baby jones I had didn't kick in until I was thirty-thousand feet in the air, and then I couldn't do anything about it.

Shannon picked me up in a taxi, and we headed to her apartment.

"What's wrong with you?" she asked.

"I think I've got a cold," I said and wiped my nose with a napkin from the airplane.

"Oh," she said, unconcerned. Shannon possessed a gift for self-involvement that rivaled even my own.

We got to her place, a shotgun apartment in the middle of the city, and I didn't even have time to unpack. She was bonkers over some guy who walked on water, and we were going snow sledding with him and his friends whether I wanted to or not. I didn't know jack about snow or sledding. This was a far cry from driving down the streets of Jacksonville looking for somebody with dope. But I was willing to do anything to stop obsessing about that particular form of recreation, so I borrowed a muffler, buttoned up my coat, piled into a car belonging to this scrawny guy, and rode through the dark Philadelphia streets to a park in German Town.

These northern guys were none too friendly, maybe because the object of Shannon's affections wasn't all that interested in her. She relentlessly pursued dudes who couldn't have cared less about her.

The city glowed a radioactive orange against the sky. The crisp air bit at my suffering nose. I stood at the top of a hill in the otherwise deserted park, watching them take turns lying belly down on the board and surfing down the sidewalk. It looked scary to me. I stamped my feet and couldn't think of anything to say to anyone, which didn't seem to be a problem since no one spoke to me anyway. Finally, Shannon insisted that I take the sled down the hill.

"Come on," she said. "It's fun." The three pale guys watched me with expressionless faces as if we were playing a poker game, and I'd just been called. Of course, if I had an accident I might have to go to the hospital and be given morphine. So I lay down on the planks, wondering where the brakes were. Then someone gave the sled a little shove, and in a few moments, I was careening down the ice. The wind skinned my face, tears streamed from my eyes and my fingers were freezing, but I was not thinking about dope for the solid two minutes that I slid down that hill and when I landed in a heap of snow, I laughed. I could beat this bad puppy.

By the third day, I began to feel sort of like a human. It hadn't been much of a habit to begin with, not with Charlie giving me little g-shots half the time.

I got a part-time job at a Roy Rogers hamburger joint and smoked hash with Shannon and her friends at night. The hash made me feel weird and paranoid, but I could never turn down drugs no matter how bad they made me feel, and it kept my mind off of Charlie. I sent him a letter, and he wrote back pages and pages of misery and regret.

After a couple of weeks, Shannon and I decided we needed to go to New Orleans for Mardi Gras. The only problem was that we had hardly any money. Shannon's parents wisely kept her on a strict allowance, and I had to spend most of my Roy Rogers earnings on our food since Shannon spent all of her money on hash and presents for the guy she liked.

"We'll hop a train," I suggested. We were sitting on the single bed in the front room of her apartment, overlooking the city street.

"Laissez les bon temps rouler," she said with a laugh.

"Fuckin' A," I answered. So we hiked over to the train yards and stared at the freight cars. How could you tell which ones were heading south? How would you know where the hell you were going? We pondered this dilemma and discussed it with her various friends and acquaintances until finally someone suggested a passenger train.

"You just hide in the bathroom until the conductor has gone through collecting tickets," the guy, a handsome, burly Black fellow, told us.

Why hadn't we thought of this ourselves? Then again, we'd never been on a train so we didn't know how it worked.

We wore several layers of clothes so we wouldn't have much to carry, a big purse for her and a small duffel bag for me. Noisy crowds of Yankees bustled hurriedly past us as if we were a couple of rocks in a stream. We walked around nervously, looking first at this train and then that one. We got on the train to New Orleans but then got scared and got back off. The train pulled away.

"This is ridiculous," Shannon said. My own fear embarrassed the hell out of me. So we boarded the next train heading south, and this time we didn't turn around. We slipped into the first bathroom we saw and found a lounge area and a tiny one-person toilet compartment. We both crammed into the compartment and locked the door. We giggled nervously. Shannon could get the funniest expressions on her face, and she kept trying to make me laugh which wasn't difficult. Then we felt a lurch, and in a moment the train began to move, slowly at first and then faster. We grimaced at each other. It was too late now to change our minds. Mardi Gras, here we come. *Les bon temps!*

The door handle jiggled; we jumped and stared at each other with wide white eyes.

"Just a moment," I called out.

We heard the perplexed voice of an old man. Shannon's brow furrowed. We had seen no signs indicating whether it was a men's room or a women's. Shannon had been to Europe once and said they had unisex bathrooms there, so that must be what this was.

After a few minutes, we decided to get out of the compartment. We opened the door slowly, peeked out. No one in the lounge area. So we sat down on the little couches and perused the magazines that we found in a pouch on the wall. There was a table, and I propped my feet up on it, flipping through a Time magazine, which was all about Tricky Dick getting a pardon. My old man gets a dime for a stereo while Nixon passes Go, collects the $200 and does not go to jail, directly or otherwise.

Another old man opened the door. He stared at us.

"It's all right. You can go ahead," I said.

"I... I thought this was the men's room," he stammered.

We shrugged. He shut the door, and Shannon and I looked at each other yet again. I'd grown familiar with each of her freckles.

"Maybe we ought to leave here," she said.

We slipped out of the restroom lounge and into the hallway. The train knocked us back and forth like pinballs as we walked. When we got into the car, we turned around. Sure enough there was the sign on the wall that said Men's Room.

"Why couldn't they have the sign on the door?" I whispered to Shannon, who started laughing so hard she could hardly walk. We sank down into a pair of empty seats. A young couple sat across the aisle from us. They had that goofball look of the freshly married — a look that Charlie and I had *never* had.

"Has the conductor come by already?" I asked the man.

"Yes," he told me. He was friendly enough with his short hair and eyes so shiny they looked like they were polished.

"Are these seats reserved?" Shannon asked. He looked at us curiously.

"Yes. Aren't those yours?" he asked.

"Um, no," I said. "Did the conductor ask to see your tickets?"

"Not yet," he said.

I glanced over at Shannon. She blinked madly.

"You don't have tickets, do you?" the guy asked.

I shook my head. He smiled in delight.

"You know," he said. "You could just go down to the club car and stay there for the whole trip. They never ask for tickets back there."

We thanked the man. He and his wife wished us good luck. They were the straightest looking couple you could imagine. I blessed their crooked little hearts.

We went back to the club car. The bartender wiped glasses and didn't pay us any mind until I sat down and cleared my throat.

"Can I get a beer?" I asked.

"You ain't 21," he said without looking up.

"I don't have to be," I answered. "I'm eighteen. Law says you can drink at 18."

He just laughed. "That's only in Florida."

"But I'm from Florida," I said.

"Whereabouts?" he asked. Turned out he was from Jacksonville, too. He and I started talking about his son, a football hero at one of the high schools. He finally let me buy the beer after I said it was for my mom. He handed the chilled glass to me with a wink.

Shannon and I found seats over by a window. I offered Shannon some of the beer, but she said she didn't feel well. In fact, her face had started to take on a green tinge.

"Hey, look over there, Shannon," I said, taking a sip of the bitter liquid.

"What?" she asked peevishly.

I pointed to two teenage girls, just a little bit younger than the two of us, who were playing cards. I nudged Shannon and walked over to them.

"Hi," I said. I guess the beer made me bold or something.

"Hi," the older one answered, noticing the glass in my hand.

"Can we play cards with you all?" I asked. I could feel Shannon behind me, her breath on the back of my neck.

"Sure," the first one said. I think we were probably the most interesting thing they'd come across on this trip. So we sat down, and I let them have sips of my beer, which I didn't like much anyway.

“Y’all know how to play poker?” I asked.

“No, we’re Catholic,” the younger one said.

Shannon and I exchanged looks.

“I’ll teach you how,” I said. The older one shrugged and handed over the deck of cards. We won eight bucks. Then the girls had to go back to their parents. They didn’t seem to mind that we’d won their money. Their folks had plenty more.

I had the universe in my pocket. All the while the expression on Shannon’s face got more sickly. My friend, the bartender, gave us two big glasses of some kind of fruity wine. Shannon took a few sips. Next thing I know she’s charging to the rest room. When she came out, she looked worse than ever. The landscape, rolling by the windows, had begun to darken.

“I think I’m pregnant,” Shannon said.

“Well, that sucks,” I said.

But we were going to Mardi Gras. We could worry about this problem later. I ate a sandwich while Shannon stared out the window at America the beautiful.

Because we’d been too frightened to take the first train to New Orleans, we had instead gotten on the one that went to Florida, which was the last place I wanted to go. We exited the train in South Carolina, spent the night in the train station and then decided to hitchhike west to New Orleans. Our trip was uneventful enough until we got to Mississippi and some big-skulled guy in a Cadillac picked us up. He looked like Billy Graham with his pouffy hair and explosive eyebrows. Only this guy didn’t have Jesus on his mind.

He asked the usual nosy questions. Then he must have noticed how overdressed we were. He had a thermostat on his dashboard. He snuck his hand down and turned up the heat. The temperature in the car climbed, and we weren’t up north anymore. I wore a velour V-neck over a turtleneck and a t-shirt under that.

“How would you girls like to make some money?” he asked.

I knew he was up to no good, but I couldn’t resist asking.

“How?”

"Just ride from here to Meridien in your bra and panties," he said. I began laughing. It was a consuming kind of laugh that I couldn't stop.

Screeeeeech. He slammed on the brakes, and I nearly flew through the windshield. The guy's nostrils flared.

"You can get out here," he said as the wheels of the caddy skidded onto the grass. I picked up my bag and kept laughing.

"Can't you at least take us to an entrance ramp?" Shannon asked. Shannon was not laughing.

"I said, get out," he repeated.

So we stepped out of the car and into the drizzle that had begun falling. The Cadillac sped off with an obligatory spray. But the fresh wet air felt good after that stultifying car. Shannon shoved me.

"Stupid. You can't laugh at people like that. What if he was a psycho? He might have killed us," Shannon said.

"If he was a real psycho, he would have killed us no matter what," I answered. I was looking down the road. Cars sped by us. I saw the one we wanted far down the highway. I don't know how I knew it was the right car, but I did. Instead of sticking my thumb out, I waved as if they were long lost friends. The red car passed us, slowed down, pulled over and backed up as we raced to it and jumped inside.

"How are y'all," a dark-haired girl in the front seat said. A perfectly built guy with a military crew cut sat in the back. Another one drove.

"God, what a great accent you have," Shannon said. "Where are you from?"

"Nu Ollins, dahlin'. We ah goin to Mawdi Graw," she said.

"So are we," I said and smiled at the guy with the military crew cut. He was, I noticed, incredibly cute and smelled good, too. I hadn't had sex since well before Charlie went to the joint. Charlie and I had never had what you would call passion-filled nights. He was always either high or looking to get high.

What can I say about Mardi Gras? The kind folks in the red car let us stay with them in a big house full of other kind people who gave us red beans and rice and beer. Turns out the two guys were Air Force pilots. That first night we all went to a concert at a place called the Warehouse. Except for pregnant Shannon who stayed back at the house and slept on the couch. The Marshall Tucker Band played. I'd never even heard of them before. The place was packed and music revved through everyone's veins. The cute Air Force pilot and I kept bumping arms. Finally, I got tired and sat down in the middle of the floor while people all around me danced, shaking their shoulders and clapping and yelling. My hand reached for a cigarette pack on the floor. I picked it up, looked inside and found a joint.

When we got back to the house, I smoked the joint with the Air Force pilot and then he lead me upstairs to a bedroom where we stripped and crawled into an empty bed. The sex was hard, no kisses, no fondling hands on the breasts. It was the kind of sex you get when a guy thinks of you as a hole and not much else. At least Charlie always whispered, I love you. I closed my eyes and went to sleep.

The next day Shannon and I took a bus downtown, and Shannon, in spite of the fact that she had this constant I'm-going-to-puke look on her face, managed to meet some rich people and get us invited to the suite of some recording company to watch the parades. Rich people attract other rich people, I've observed.

We hung out on the balcony and collected a mass of colorful plastic beads that we wore on our necks, our wrists and even our ankles. Even Shannon was finally having a good time. About midnight we staggered out of the hotel, laughing but thinking we'd better get back to the house where we'd left our stuff. The streets were thronged with characters that emerged from hallucinatory dreams, everyone drunk on hurricanes, screaming and laughing like hyenas.

A hand grabbed me by the shoulder. I pulled away, but the hand grabbed me again.

"Trish," a voice said. I turned around. Shannon did, too.

"Oh no," Shannon said. Then I saw him, shirtless and pock-marked face, my old chum from Jacksonville, Jasper Collins.

"Hi, Trish. Hi, Shannon," Jasper said. The motherless son of an Episcopal priest, Jasper had always, without fail, gotten me into trouble. Like the time we almost got suspended for smoking a joint in the supply room by the football field in the eleventh grade. Fortunately, the teacher who saw us thought we'd gone in there to make-out. Her mistake kept us out of serious trouble but was infinitely more embarrassing.

I hugged him. He was the first person besides Shannon I'd seen from home in about a month, and I guess I didn't realize how homesick I'd been.

Jasper didn't waste time catching up on the bad old days.

"Y'all wanna buy a Dilaudid?" he asked.

"No," Shannon said, but I didn't even blink.

"How much?" I asked.

"Ten for you," he said, which meant ten for anyone.

"I don't have any works," I said.

Jasper sighed and rolled his eyes.

"All right. I got an extra set I'll give you," he said. People jostled around us, screaming and calling out to each other.

I did have ten bucks. Just ten bucks. But I'd heard the call, and it was insistent. Dilaudids gave as good a high as heroin. Actually, a little better since they were made by the demi-gods of the pharmaceutical industry and therefore always clean, always pure.

Shannon reluctantly followed me as I hurried after Jasper to a flashy white Camaro around the corner. I felt a surge of power, the power to throw everything good away. No one can stop you from self-destructing. No one.

"Here you go," he said, dropping a tiny white pill in my hand and an old set of works. We had no water, so I couldn't get off in the car, but Jasper was kind enough to drive us back to the house off in the Garden District where our Air Force friends were staying.

The front door of the two-story wooden house was unlocked. They'd said it was all right for us to stay another night. We weren't the only ones from out of town making ourselves at home. But nearly everyone else was gone or asleep. Shannon found a bed and fell into it exhausted. I realized I didn't ever want to get pregnant if that's what it was like. What if I'd had a baby with Charlie? The idea was too terrible to contemplate. I found a bathroom, poured some water into the barrel of the syringe, dropped in the Dilaudid and started shaking it madly. I'd done Dilaudids once before with Charlie, and I had memorized the steps. In a second the needle was in my vein. In another second I had answered the call. The drug and I were one.

About five the next morning, the guy who owned the house was shaking me awake from the chair where I had nodded off. I looked up groggily. Shannon stood next to him, looking guilty and a little frightened.

"This your needle?" the guy asked me. I stared at him stupidly. He held exhibit A in the palm of his hand. "I already asked your friend and she says it isn't hers."

I looked at Shannon, who was trying to smile at the guy and glare at me at the same time. Of course, they'd suspect her first what with her looking sick and wanting to sleep all the time. I shook my head.

"You girls better leave," he said. His wife or girlfriend stood in the doorway of the kitchen with crossed arms and a cat-spitting look on her mug.

"All right," I said. I found the bag with my stuff in it. I wanted to use the bathroom but thought better of it. Shannon grabbed her things and shot me a look that could have carried a bullet. We went outside. It was chilly and damp.

We started walking silently along the sidewalk.

Finally, Shannon stopped near a picket fence and threw up. Then she looked at me with tears in her eyes.

"This is just fucking great," she said.

I shrugged, guilty as charged.

We went to a park, sat down and waited for the sun to rise. I figured since we were broke we should hitchhike to Jacksonville since it was so much closer than Philadelphia. Her parents would surely fly her back to school.

"Fuck you. I'm tired," Shannon said and buried her face in her hands.

She didn't seem to want to do anything. I wandered around the park while she sat on a bench and sulked. I thought about panhandling enough to get us some food. But there was hardly anyone around. Shannon probably wouldn't have been able to eat anyway.

But the universe still nestled in my pocket, and this is how I know. It must have been about 8:30 in the morning. I'd walked around the block a couple of times and wound up back in the park. There on a bench sat a pocketbook, the kind that stands up on its own with the short stiff handle, the kind that old ladies carry. I stared at the pocketbook. No one was around except Shannon who'd finally joined up with me. Providence had been true to its name and provided. I slipped my fingers around the handle of that pocketbook, found the nearest bathroom and locked myself in a stall. In the wallet, I found $138.

Shannon stood outside the stall.

"How much?" she asked in a breathless voice.

"Enough for an abortion," I told her. I tucked thirty dollars in my bra, opened the door and handed her a hundred bucks. Then I waved the other eight dollars. "And we can get a couple of beignets before we start thumbing home."

Shannon grabbed the money, hugged me, and kissed me on the cheek.

It took us only two rides to get to Jacksonville. The first one was a bunch of hippies in a VW van that took us as far as Pensacola. A scrawny long-haired guy who smiled too much kept telling me I was the most beautiful girl he'd ever seen. I looked all right. I had interesting eyes, according to most people, and a decent body, but Cover Girl wasn't calling me, and neither was Playboy. Guys seem to think that when they tell a girl she's beautiful, she'll simply roll over and spread her legs. Like being beautiful is the dog biscuit we're all craving. Well, I wasn't going to fuck this guy for anything in the world. They let us off on I-10 at Pensacola. The next ride was a garrulous old truck driver who dropped us off a few blocks from my mom's apartment. She wasn't there, but I knew where the extra key was hidden. While Shannon took a shower, I found the keys to my Mazda and finally felt like a real person again instead of an indentured slave to the hard dicks of the world.

I took Shannon to have her abortion the next day and then drove her to the airport that night. She looked like she'd been dragged behind an automobile. I pulled up to the sky cap but she had nothing to check.

"Take care of yourself," she said, not really meaning it.

"You, too," I answered. Then I drove away without waiting for her to get on the plane. I still had some money. I headed downtown.

I was nodding out on the couch in front of the TV at my mom's when she came home.

"Hello," she called out.

"Hi," I mumbled.

I accidentally looked up at her. She stared at my glassy pinpoint pupil eyes. Her shoulders slumped and her face fell like an avalanche.

"Oh, Trish," she said.

Trouble Man

I had returned to my old room with clean sheets on the bed and the baby blue princess phone on my nightstand. I took a part-time job as the afternoon receptionist at a dentist's office, thinking he might have drugs, but he didn't. I also took some college courses at the community college.

Every once in a while, I would slowly cruise through an apartment complex, pick some place that looked empty, park and go knock on the door. If no one came, I slid the screw-driver out of my pocket and jammed it into the door lock. I wasn't particularly big or strong—110 pounds, five foot four, but with the right leverage, I could sometimes get the door open if they didn't use a deadbolt. The first time one opened for me, I was so startled and frightened that I walked in, turned around, and went right back out without taking anything. After I got a little braver, I'd tiptoe about like a ghost, using a Kleenex or a paper towel to open the drawers, check for cash or guns, anything that would be easy to trade. Nothing big, but not jewelry unless it was diamonds. No one wants another cheap watch.

It didn't even occur to me to wonder why I didn't have friends. I'd had friends in high school, but they'd all gone off to college or jobs, those regular lives that seemed elusive and incomprehensible. Me, I'd slipped into some other dimension. Time stood still, watching to see what I'd do next. I investigated those apartments as if I was searching for my life. Sometimes I'd take something very small, a picture, a toothbrush, a can opener, a tube of lipstick. I kept these objects in a shoebox as mementos of the ordinary world.

One day I spent the morning driving around town, waiting for that nerve to rise within me. I had cramps from my period, I was schizoid with boredom, and getting high seemed the most honorable undertaking. Before long, I'd found an apartment complex where no one was wandering around outside.

I am inside—looks like the place belongs to Bachelor Number One. Empty Bud cans on the kitchen counter and a Domino's box full of pizza crusts on the table. Generic vinyl brown furniture, some hunting magazines and a *Playboy*. I go into the bedroom and open up the night table.

A sound! A key in a lock. The front door opens. Shit! I look down and see a .357 magnum sitting in the drawer. I reach in, pluck the gun from the drawer and slide the drawer back shut. Then I lie down on the floor and scoot under the bed. I hear him come in the room. Hear footsteps on the other side of the bed. A dresser drawer opens. I'm thinking to myself, whatever happens I am not going to shoot this gun. I am going to lie my way out of this. Tell him I thought my husband lived here with another woman. A voice in my head says, "Tell him anything."

But the gun is in my hand, and my heart has stopped pounding. I'm not breathing. I float in some strange vortex in time, noticing the box springs under the bed, the striped sheet dangling on the side, the belt coiled under the bed, the dust balls on the floor. It reminds me of when I was a kid doing a routine on the uneven bars, that moment when I'd be in a handstand high up in the air, that moment before gravity called and I would swing back down. I hear the footsteps leave the room. The front door opens and shuts.

I sit up and look around. Empty. Then I start shaking. I get up quickly. The dresser drawer is still open. I look in. Marijuana. Shit. Did he come home to get a joint? Or to deposit the goods? I reach in to take it and then I don't. I am so grateful that he hadn't walked all the way around the bed I have to leave him something. So I take the gun, which is probably worth at least six bags of dope, and slip it into my jacket, and I split, somehow thinking I've done the guy a favor.

As I drive across the bridge to the other side of town, I pretend I am Mata Hari, heading toward the border with stolen state secrets. I feel so happy, so singular. I could be Batman, I think. All I need is the cape.

I sat in my car just outside of downtown Jacksonville on a sandy road behind a subdivision of nice little brick houses where only Black folks lived. A spring storm had left rain puddles in the ruts of the road. The air smelled like clean glass. I waited for Train to bring me three bags of dope. Train had the best dope in town. Everyone knew this. I had 24 dollars instead of 25, because it was standard procedure to cop short though Train would sometimes tell you that you couldn't cop short that day. He tended to let me cop short. I was the only white female I knew of that ever came down that way by herself.

A Toyota pulled up next to me, a dark-haired, good-looking guy behind the wheel. His eyes were the color of Coca-Cola as he stared at me. I stared right back.

"Hey," he said, hanging out the window. "Is Train straight?"

I shrugged. I couldn't place this dude. But he seemed to know me.

"You got some place to get off?" he asked.

I shook my head.

"You can get off at my chick's place after you cop," he said.

Train was short with chocolate-brown skin. He never smiled. He loped up and dropped three bags into the palm of my hand which was hanging out the window.

"Y'all need to hurry and get outta here," he said. "All this traffic is gonna bring the heat." He sold some dope to the dark-haired guy, and I finally figured out who he was when I overheard Train call him "my man, Timothy." Timothy Jones—a name I'd heard though I couldn't exactly remember the context. I did recollect he was the son of somebody who owned an appliance store or something.

"Coming?" he asked.

I followed him, and we wound up in a garage apartment that belonged to this girl he was seeing. She had delicate features, long bleached-blond hair and looked like she could have been a model. In fact, she seemed to pose as she watched us in our preparations. She leaned against the wall and then strode around the table and sprawled on the couch. Then she sat up again and gazed at her red fingernails.

"And so who is this girl, Timmy?" she asked.

"Just a friend," Timothy answered.

"A friend, Timmy?" She tossed her mane of hair and glared at me, as if I should fall to my knees at the mere sight of such pouty gorgeousness.

I took the needle from Timothy and found the secret password to the land of golden treasures. The dope was good and smooth as baby oil. Timothy's lips looked like they were melting. The girlfriend started cleaning up our stuff. She opened the blinds and the light came blasting in like an army of beams.

"I gotta go, man," I told him. "Your chick is fucking up my high."

Timothy nodded, tossed the girlfriend the keys to her car and left with me. She posed tragically against the window as we drove away.

Timothy and I were a good match. We weren't in love or anything, but we made a helluva team, and we managed to run enough scams to get off just about every day, maybe taking something to the pawn shop or copping dope for some rich white kid and cutting the bags in half or running some ten-dollar change scams at a few liquor stores. We fucked occasionally but it was more for the sake of form than for any real enjoyment, which is how it had been with Charlie as well. I had no idea if sex was something I actually would like.

We were only together a few weeks when his buddy Big Steve rolled into town from California. The California junkies seemed more real than the rest of us because California dope was so much better. We could hardly get a habit on Cowford dope these days.

I'd quit my job at the dentist office, but Timothy and Big Steve took jobs in one of the shipyards, doing construction. I parked at the edge of the construction site not fifty yards from a humongous battle-gray boat that looked like it was made shortly after the Merrimac. I leaned against the front fender of my car, waiting for them to get off work. I hadn't met Big Steve yet, but I'd heard about him for years.

Finally I saw them, loping toward me, in T-shirts and ripped up Levis, spattered with drywall putty. Big Steve wore a red bandanna over his hair. Underneath that bandanna and the splotches on his clothes, he was as beautiful a man as I had ever seen. He had a thick mustache framing his full lips, and his eyes were green as rye grass. He could have been the Sundance Kid.

"Big Steve's like my brother, Trish," Timothy said, clapping Big Steve on the shoulder. "He is just like my bro. He just did 18 months in Chino."

"What the hell is Chino?"

"It's a prison in California," Big Steve said in an easy nonchalant voice. "It's not too bad. Got a lot of reading done."

"Who's that guy you're always talking about?" Timothy asked Big Steve.

"Nietzsche," he answered. He had a little half-suppressed smile on his face as if he found everything Timothy did slightly amusing.

"Nietzsche?" I asked, "No shit." All I knew of Nietzsche was that his name was on a book in the bookshelf at home—leftover from my father, or maybe it belonged to my brother. The titles were *The Twilight of the Gods* and *The Anti-Christ*. Must have belonged to my father.

"He's all right, but I like the Buddhists better," Big Steve said, shoving his hands in his pockets, looking around. A truck rumbled by, and the man inside waved at us. Big Steve waved back.

"Yeah," Timothy said, kicking a stone. "Big Steve believes in reincarnation. He thinks that when you die, you come back and have to live another life."

"I know what reincarnation is," I said, taking a cigarette from Timothy's fingers and inhaling. "It makes as much sense as anything else, I guess."

"I just hope there's plenty of dope in all my lives," Timothy said.

"Man, you could be a cockroach in your next life," Big Steve said.

"The better to get into someone's dope."

Big Steve turned his eyes toward me and studied me for the first time. I felt like he was wearing X-ray glasses, and it made me nervous.

"You still married to Charlie?" he asked.

"Technically."

"His loss . . ." Timothy began.

"Is our gain," Big Steve finished. They laughed and then Timothy shrugged.

"I hate to see anyone doing that much time," he said. But I got the feeling he didn't much like Charlie. Junkies had their cliques and rivalries just like anyone else.

The reincarnation theory held water with me. What else could explain the strange inevitability of this life? I imagined us as disembodied souls, former gunslingers and train robbers—Timothy, Big Steve, me, and Charlie, too —congregating in the place where souls meet to discuss their next lives, to plan our meetings. What was our secret sign, the signal that identified us to each other in this plane? An unconscious tic? A smell? A peculiar shrug of the shoulder? Of course, we were botching it badly in this go-round. The test might be simply whether or not we escaped hanging this time around.

When Timothy and Big Steve finished work for the day, we copped a few bags from Train and drove toward Big Steve's mom's house. A freight train came barreling down the tracks on our way back home, and we knew it would hang us up for hours.

"Go around the barricade before it gets here, Trish," Timothy said.

I looked down the track. I could hear the train horn blowing. I threw the car into low gear and took off.

"Holy shit," Big Steve said. He was probably thinking about what he wanted to be in his next life.

Fifteen minutes later we all had trickles of blood dripping down our arms, and we were greasy.

In back of her house, Big Steve's mom had an addition built with jalousie windows and a magnolia tree outside. She let Big Steve stay there for free, and we could come and go because it had its own separate door. It was like a little boy's room in a way. A bunk bed, high school baseball trophies and games—Monopoly, Clue and Scrabble—stacked up on the shelves. Big Steve once had a younger brother. I went to junior high school with him—a real sweet guy who was kind of cute and never had anything nasty to say about anyone else. He was riding his bicycle when an older lady drove into him and crushed his neck. Big Steve's father was also dead. He died in Vietnam when Steve was 13.

"He was one of the first casualties," Big Steve told me one night when we were playing Scrabble. He had just scored big with the word "quiz."

"Does it still bother you?" I wanted to know.

"I'm not attached to life," Big Steve said. I knew what he meant, but I couldn't say it was true for me. In spite of everything, I wanted to live. Even though an animal lurked inside me howling to get out, even though I felt whacko most of the time and barely resisted the urge to slice open my blood tunnels, even though a raw pain that came from some hidden cave inside me swarmed around my psyche like angry flies, I had another voice in my head—one that told me to hang on no matter what. I wondered if enough of this lowdown life would silence that voice.

Timothy and Big Steve and I took up residence in Big Steve's room. Timothy's ex-girlfriend and his ex-wife joined forces and came by and harassed us on a daily basis. They called Timothy several times a day.

"Just tell me something, please," his ex-wife would beg on the phone.

"What do you want me to tell you, Cynthia?" Timothy asked.

I pulled the phone away from him and heard her say, "You know what I want to hear."

Then I hung up the phone.

"What is with her?" I asked Timothy.

"We got together she was 16," he said. "I wish she'd find someone else. I'm no good for her."

I looked at him, studied his pretty face, the long eyelashes, soft cheeks. I figured if I had fallen in love with him when I was 16, I would still have wanted him too, I guess. But I fell in love with heroin, which had made life both easier and harder.

Later Cynthia and the ex-girlfriend came by and sat in the driveway, leaning on the horn. Then they tore out of there, trying to leave rubber on the white driveway. Big Steve laughed.

Timothy was always talking up Big Steve to me—how brilliant he was, how he could have gone to officer's school for the Air Force. Big Steve never bragged. Life was a tilt-a-whirl ride for him. He was so affable, nothing could piss him off. I wondered if that's what the Buddhists were like. I couldn't get that detachment without a needle, but then he seemed to need the drug, too. Or perhaps, he didn't need it. Perhaps he was just testing the limits of life, examining the boundaries.

The three of us took off in my Mazda to Daytona Beach for Easter weekend. Timothy and I brought a bunch of bunk: fake LSD. I hated scamming people. I always wound up liking them and feeling shitty about their excitement, the way they thought they were going to be getting high. I used to like acid myself when I was about fifteen. But I didn't feel bad enough to stop scamming them.

When we first got to the beach, we drove on the wide sandy expanse, passing rows of parked cars, sun hanging like a grapefruit on the horizon. A police cruiser followed, telling people to get their cars off the beach, which was off limits for cars after sunset. Pretty soon all that was left was a golden haze.

"I wish the roller wasn't on our ass," Timothy said, looking in the rearview mirror at the cop car, as he turned off the beach and headed north along A1A. I glanced behind us and saw the bubble lights.

“Don’t look back at him,” Big Steve said. I turned to the front, obediently, and looked straight ahead. The things you had to give up for this life annoyed me more than I would ever say. I could feel the bars coming down: you can’t look at cops, you can’t be friends with anyone outside of your partners, you can’t show any pity for a chump. How tiresome it could be.

My car backfired, and Timothy said, “You gotta get that fixed, Trish.”

"Sure, man, sure. Can we please go to the Steak 'N' Shake," I whined.

"You're hungry?" he asked.

"Yes, I am. Besides we won't be able to eat later." Our habits weren’t bad enough to send us writhing on the ground, begging God for a fix, but we’d be feeling pukey and miserable soon, and we all knew it was coming the way birds know when to expect a hurricane. Besides, we could afford a few burgers.

"She's right. We better eat," Big Steve advised. Timothy shrugged his shoulders and turned the car around. He liked driving, so I almost always let him even though it was my car.

Inside the glove compartment there was a baggie full of placebo birth control pills from all my old packages--the pink inactive ones which help women stay on the cycle. We had rubbed off the pharmaceutical logos with an emery board so they were blank and innocuous. In another baggie, we had about 100 gelatin caps that were filled with light brown sugar. The birth control pills, we called acid. The caps we called mescaline. Big Steve also had a couple bags of reefer for sale.

In the Steak 'N' Shake I got a chocolate milkshake and fries. Big Steve got a hamburger all the way, fries and a coke. Timothy got a coke and a cheeseburger. We sat down at the red table to eat, and Timothy squeezed my shoulder. Timothy liked to play lover-boy. I guess it worked with those chicks who still mooned for him. Though technically speaking I was his girl, I'd never mooned over him, and that's probably why he liked me.

Night time. The crowded streets smell of stale spilled beer. Everywhere are neon signs, Harleys, girls in bikini tops and shorts, guys puking. Timothy and I sit on a bus bench watching the action when some drunks drive by us singing "Free Bird" at the top of their soused lungs. Timothy and I have made some "ends" but not enough. We need at least a hundred bucks if we're going to buy a half load, which is eleven bags of dope. Anything less is pointless—the dope in Cowford is so trashy. Timothy and I both have little chippers, small habits, but habits nonetheless. Big Steve is no good at beating people—selling bunk. That's why he's brought a couple bags of genuine marijuana to sell. The money isn't as good, but you don't have to be Ethel Merman on Broadway. The performance, of course, was the attraction for Timothy, and probably for me, too. The challenge of selling absolutely nothing at all.

"I'm going to buy a beer," Timothy says. I look at him like he's lost his mind, and he leaves me in the neon light of the bar while he goes inside. Three reeling drunks pass by me, calling, "Pussy! Pussy! Pussy! Meow."

I feel a wave of relief when I see Big Steve crossing the street.

"I sold a bag," he says in a whisper. Timothy comes out with a Budweiser and sits on the other side of me. When he puts the cold can against my arm, I jump away from him. He laughs, takes a sip, then grimaces.

"Want some?" he asks. I shake my head.

"Hey, man," Big Steve says. "This place is loaded with chumps."

"Yeah, but they're all drunk," Timothy says and spits beer on the sidewalk. Four or five college kids ride by real slow in a shiny orange firebird.

"Buy some drugs?" Timothy calls out. One of them leans out the window and pukes as they drive on. "See what I mean."

"That's disgusting," Big Steve says. Then he peers over at some bikers just down the street, standing on the corner. "I'll be right back."

I drape an arm over Timothy and watch as Big Steve goes over to them. Big Steve pushes the hair out of his face and shakes one of the biker's hands. The biker has muscles bulging under his tattoos. He has a scraggly beard; a chain connects his wallet to his belt. A few minutes later, Big Steve walks by me but doesn't look at me.

"Come over to that parking lot," he says. "But don't let those guys see you." Junkies are naturally wary of bikers. In the animal kingdom, we'd be the coyotes and they'd be the wolverines. I wait until he goes, then nonchalantly walk to the corner of the street and cross over to the parking lot where he's waiting. We stroll behind a car, and I hand him the bag of reefer that I'd kept in my purse.

"Stay back a few minutes, girl," Big Steve says and gives my arm a little squeeze. "Okay?" His voice wraps around me. I have this flash of memory of my older brother carrying me piggy-back across our backyard so I wouldn't step on sand spurs.

I hang back as Big Steve strides across the gravel and goes around the building where the bikers are waiting. Then I stroll onto the street and stand next to a little grocery store, which is doing a brisk business in beer and Zigzag rolling papers. I slowly walk along the sidewalk, watching Big Steve in the street near five parked Harleys. Then the muscular biker and he start across the street. I'm about ten yards to the right when I see the gun poking into Big Steve's back. A rip-off! Adrenaline hits my system like a shot of crystal meth.

Some people pass between us, talking loudly and laughing. I stumble into the street through the crowd, thinking there's nothing to do except let the robbery go down, but I can already feel a trembling in my legs. Then Big Steve stops just on the other side of the street and the muscular biker screams at him and shoves something in his face. Then someone else pushes Big Steve against a car and yanks his hands behind his back. Cops! Who would have thought you'd find cops under those scraggly beards? It almost wasn't fair.

Two surfers come up and stand next to me.

"Bummer," one of the surfers says.

In a minute I am standing in the middle of the road alone as people scatter, and a burly guy jams Big Steve into the back seat of a car. When Big Steve glances out of the window, our eyes lock. Then the car drives off.

Timothy and I sleep on the beach that night. Thank God, he doesn't want to fuck is all I can think. I'm so lonely I wish I'd fall asleep and never wake up. But I can't fall asleep. My back aches. The hard sand rolls under me like tiny metal ball bearings. The night is long, long, long. Finally I doze, and when I do, I dream of an old man in a long black coat, who takes me into a cathedral full of stained glass windows, but each window is a scene of torture—naked people being burned by demons, the tips of their penises or nipples held by prongs. The old man takes me to a narrow stairwell, leading down to I don't know where. I'm afraid to follow, but can't help myself. I go into the stairwell and everything is dark. When I wake up, the dream lingers in my mouth like the taste of metal. I am going to hell and I'm not even dead yet.

In the morning we go to the police station and wait outside for Big Steve to be let out on his own recognizance. He finally comes shambling out. Big Steve and Timothy slap each other's backs and call each other "brother." I don't say much of anything, but I'm happy just to see him out in the sugary morning light.

"Do you have to come back to court?" I ask Big Steve.

He laughs.

"Are you crazy, girl? I can't come back here. I'm on parole in California," he says. Timothy looks at me as if I've gone stupid like one of those chicks who sniffed way too much glue and have white paste for brains.

We headed back toward the beach, and spent the day selling bunk to whomever was trusting and foolish enough to buy. Big Steve lay on a towel, trying to make up for lost sleep.

In the middle of the day, I wandered into the warm waves for some body surfing. I pointed my arms in front of me, pushed off at the right moment, and the wave rumbled over me, bubbling around my head and tossing me into the sand in the shallows. The rough sand against my chest and stomach made me feel less achy. I rolled over, sank back and let a smaller wave neatly plaster my hair away from my face. I shook the sand from my bikini before I stood and looked for the car. Timothy and Big Steve leaned against it, watching me.

It was late afternoon, cars parked all over Daytona Beach, a few people packing up. I sat on the metal railing of the Boardwalk, feeling the last rays of the spring sun on my back. I had about forty bucks in the pocket of my cut offs when a guy with a long pony-tail who bought some bogus mescaline the night before came up to me and said, "Hey, that shit wasn't any good."

I sniffled, feeling ragged, but I feigned surprise.

"I want my money," he said.

"I don't have it," I said. "But my boyfriend has some more mescaline. Maybe you just got a bad hit." My gut twisted around this lie, and the impulse to tell him the truth had to be slapped down hard. What I wanted to do was get him to Timothy quick before I broke weak and handed him back his cash.

"I don't want any more," he said in a reasonable voice.

I slid down off the railing.

"All right," I said, rubbing the back of my neck. "Let's go find my boyfriend."

He followed me down some wooden steps onto the soft white sand of the beach. My feet sank with every step as he trundled wordless behind me. Timothy stood near the wet line of the shore. He looked out of place on the beach in his jeans and his T-shirt, his longish dirty hair. As I got near him, I could smell the sweat from a night and a day on the beach.

"This guy wants his money back," I said.

"Your girlfriend sold me some bad stuff," the pony-tail guy said.

Timothy looked at him just briefly and then slid his arm into mine and said, "All right. Follow me." Then we walked past the guy back toward the boardwalk.

I had no idea where we were going or what we were going to do. I felt myself shaking, but Timothy took my hand and squeezed it. The dude was right behind us. We passed the little arcades and shops by the boardwalk. Then we stopped in front of a pink two-story motel.

Timothy turned around and said without really looking at the guy, "Our room is in here, man. Wait here and I'll go get your money."

"Okay, but your girlfriend stays here," the dude said, arms crossed over his tank top.

Timothy glanced at me.

"Sorry. I can't," I said. "I gotta pee."

We both turned and walked through a small hallway. I saw Timothy grab a beer bottle from the floor of the hallway. Then he pulled me behind me a coke machine. My heart hammered as I heard the guy calling down the hallway.

"Hey, man, give me a refund!" the guy said, his voice trying to pull us back.

When he walked past us, Timothy moved in behind him and pushed the lip of the beer bottle into his back. I followed Timothy and looked anxiously around to see if anyone was going to accidentally join this little drama.

"This is a .44, motherfucker. Get down on the ground," Timothy said in a hard voice. I looked on in disbelief as the guy dropped to his knees and sank down to the ground.

"Don't shoot me, man," the guy said, his voice cracking like ice hitting the floor. "Please don't kill me."

"You stay here. You stay right here for 15 minutes," Timothy said. "If I see you again, I'll blow your fucking head off. And if you go to the cops, I'll tell them you're the dope dealer."

Then we backed out of the hallway, and a few minutes later we were heading back to the boardwalk. I began to laugh the way someone laughs at a horror movie right after the scary part.

At that moment my apprenticeship ended. Up until then I had thought of myself as the honest, basically good-hearted person I had been before I ever stuck a needle in my arm. I was the person who would skip school in order to spend the day in a car with someone, talking them down from a bad trip. I believed in peace and love, etc. But as we walked away that afternoon, I was fully complicit. I had completed my metamorphosis. The electricity surged through my muscles, and the creature inside me came to life. I was a junkie in every sense of the word. Better to be a junkie than a victim, I thought. But I also had a bad feeling that someday we were gonna pay for scaring the piss out of that poor guy.

The First Time

The first time I ever shot heroin I was still in high school. I was driving around town by myself, having just broken up with my boyfriend of six months, who had screamed at me during P.E. the day before for skipping study hall to go 'shroom hunting with Jasper Collins. I drove past the Dobbs House where my old boyfriend was eating pecan pie with a green-haired girl on the swim team. I looked in at them and thought, better you than me, babe; then I drove on and pulled up to the park by the river where the seniors drank beer and sat on picnic tables, making noises but saying nothing at all. Jasper Collins was there, selling Quaaludes. I sat on the hood of my car, staring at the Spanish moss. Then an older guy, whose name I'll never remember, came up and asked if I wanted to do some smack.

"You bet," I said as if he'd just invited me to fly to the moon.

I went with him and another girl to a duplex. We took our turns, holding out our arms for the hummingbird kiss. It felt like cashmere coating the inside of my body. I knew for the first time that I was in pieces and that this substance melded the pieces back together. They say the first shot is free, but it wasn't. I gave him ten bucks and thanked him. Then I stepped into a new reality, one that was obedient and comforting. I was a knight who'd found her armor.

Water Music

When I was about seven, Mom and I moved from our little house with the weedy lawn to an upstairs apartment with a thick door and two deadbolts. I was distraught to leave a neighborhood full of kids for a musty old place in Riverside where the average age of the residents was 92.

"I need some security," she said. "A safe place."

This is why: A man had kicked down the back door of our little house on the south side. He had dragged my screaming mother outside and raped her while I ran, barefoot and terrified, to the neighbor's house to get help. The neighbors called the police, and when the sirens broke through the neighborhood quiet, the man, who had threatened to kill my mother, got up and ran away. That's the story in a nut graph as the journalists say. But the repercussions of that one night lasted my mother's lifetime. Even when she was an old woman, she would often cry out in terror in the middle of the night.

And what did it mean to that seven-year-old child, who had woken up to hear her mother screaming, "Fire! Fire!" to the operator because she thought that was the only way to get help? Or when the kid who lived across the street said, "My parents heard your mom screaming but they didn't do anything because they thought your dad had come back." You don't need a degree in psychology to understand the rage that was born in my heart that night. That night the girl junkie who was willing to destroy herself as long as she took someone else with her was born.

What I also came to understand was that my mother no longer got any child support or alimony from my father, that she'd taken him to court and it had done no good, that he called sometimes drunk and threatening. I surmised these things from fragments of overheard conversations.

Although loneliness plagued me, the years in the upstairs apartment in Riverside were not bad. I rode my bike in solitary wanderings and found places--behind churches or along the waterfront—that I made my own. In the backyard there was a pecan tree and a grassy area underneath it where I sometimes took naps. We had a wild garden filled with azalea bushes, morning glory vines and tall white lilies.

Beside the house was a tall delicate mimosa tree with pink blooms in summer that looked like fairy ballerinas. Afternoons I would climb into that mimosa tree and let the branches cradle me. In spring, large translucent nests of caterpillars created cottony castles in the farthest reaches of the branches. I would stare at the nests, watching the barely visible forms of the caterpillars which would soon be everywhere, orange and black and fuzzy. The image of that web-like world haunted me for years.

Inside I played with my marbles and my plastic horses, frozen in various states of running or bucking, while Mom practiced her piano for hours or gave voice lessons to members of the church choir, where my mother was music director.

My mother said she felt like a bird in that apartment, that treehouse of ours. She placed suet and sunflower seeds in a tray feeder outside her window for blue jays, cardinals and grey-coated mockingbirds. Sometimes in spring we'd get red-winged blackbirds like messengers from heaven.

She played in the symphony, at a huge Episcopal church, and for local community theaters. We listened to records of Vivaldi, Mozart, the Brandenburg concertos, Handel's Water Music. Sometimes she composed. I remember parties at our apartment where people came and drank and talked and laughed hour upon hour. My mother said she loved the life of the mind. Later I understood that the heart was a scary place for her.

Then she met Richie.

Richie worked as a high-school chorus teacher. He was funny and sweet, and the corners of his eyes crinkled when he smiled. He was younger than my mom. He never went to the opera. Richie was not an alcoholic. He had been raised a Baptist, but he was trying to shed the stigma, and he wouldn't talk much about it.

"He's not a drinker like the rest of them," Mom confided in me. She didn't drink much herself.

Even then my best friend was Shannon. Our addiction? Mosquito poison. We followed behind the mosquito truck on our bicycles, lost and laughing as billowy grey curtains surrounded us.

One night after it had come wafting by, Shannon and I placed my life-size doll--about as big as a three-year-old child--in the middle of the road under the thick toxin, her hard plastic body smeared with ketchup. We watched giggling, panicky in the gut, from my upstairs bedroom window, lights off, huddled, looking down, as the cars came slowly moving through the fog. Then we heard the sharp squeal of brakes, and we squeezed each other's hands. We could see figures moving in the toxic shadows, heard the slam of car doors. When the first group of cars moved on, we rushed back outside. The doll was gone, and the night was a grey smear in front of my face. I remembered that the doll had been a Christmas present from my mother, and I suddenly wanted it back. It must have been the first time in my life I felt regret—not for what we had done, for I surely couldn't understand the confusion or fear the driver of that car must have felt, but for losing something I hadn't realized was important—no, not for losing it, but for throwing it away just for the sake of a dissipating thrill.

Across the street from my school was a library, painted the color of lime sherbet. Granite steps led up to the glass doors. Beside the steps were concrete railings just wide enough for a kid's butt to go sliding down in the hot summer afternoon. I spent hours in the library.

Inside it was cool; the beams of the high ceilings carved in a rococo design. I would follow a small narrow staircase down to the children's section to find *The Black Stallion, The Black Stallion Returns*, all the novels of Walter Farley that I read and believed in, a kid on an island with no one to love but a black horse. I browsed the adult section, too. Just wandering, touching the backs of books as if I knew them and it would be unkind not to acknowledge them.

One time Shannon and I got kicked out of the library for our rowdy behavior--our loud hyena laughter. So we crossed the street and wandered the maze of prize rose bushes that belonged to the Garden Club. We dallied by the enormous blossoms, yellow and pink and red with petals so thick and curvaceous you wanted to run your tongue along them. I buried my face in those flowers and intoxicated myself with their pungency. Our fingers ran along the stems, testing the thorns, thrilling at the tiny prick of pain. Then before we knew it, the roses were gathered into our hands like beating hearts, and we were running home along the sidewalks, under the leafy shade of magnolias, mimosas, oaks, sweet gum and crepe myrtles past the big red brick houses, the white wooden houses, and the stucco apartment buildings, dodging the cars as we dashed across the streets, sunbeams shooting at us from windshields, all the while our treasure clasped to our chests, sprinkling drops of blood from our fingers like holy water.

My mother's eyes widened when I handed her the roses.

"They're gorgeous," she said, and then gave me a look, an odd combination of pleasure and disapproval that told me she knew just where I had gotten them.

I wanted the frog legs. It was after their wedding at the Justice of the Peace, and we had gone to a French restaurant to celebrate. I asked for frog legs. Richie smiled and told me I could have anything I wanted on the menu and that the reason French people were called “Frogs” was because they loved to eat the scrawny little amphibians.

"Tastes like chicken," he said. His eyes crinkled. He was my new dad, and we were mad for each other. I liked the way he smelled of cigarette smoke, the way his voice was soft, never, ever loud, that smile that seemed to come from way down inside him like the last dregs in a bottle of root beer.

Mother laughed. She was giddy. I didn't like her so much -- not the way she was with Richie. She had always been so sure of herself, so sure of everything, she who read books and could quote Emily Dickinson or discuss atonal musical theory, she whose infectious laughter could melt hearts, she who could make people sing just by raising her hands. Now, she deferred to him and seemed like someone else altogether, but I would put up with this new mother for the sake of having a father.

"Do you really want frog legs?" she asked.

"That's what I said, isn't it?" I said. "Frog legs."

After Mom and Richie got married, we moved to a red-brick, two-story house on Park Street. Mother loved the place. She stripped decades worth of grime off the floors and revealed a parquet wood pattern. She tore down the wallpaper and painted the walls ivory. She varnished the banister and laid carpet on the stairs. Richie and I watched the house transform under her frantic attentions. I liked the house, too, but I never felt at home there. I had picked lousy decor for my room—a bright red bedspread, black and white curtains. It looked all right in my mind, but in real life, it made me feel like I was in a zoo.

Mom took Richie to her parties; when they came home, he was edgy. He smoked more. How could you take an altar boy, which is how I thought of him even then, to those parties and expect him to fit in? Richie started drinking screwdrivers at the parties. I knew because I got to serve when the parties were at our house.

Richie came in one day and found me in the Florida room, a sunny room at the front of the house with wicker furniture. I was engrossed in my D'aulaire's Mythology, but looked up to see him. He winked at me.

"I've got a surprise," he said. I dropped the book to the floor and sprang up. The novelty of having a father had not worn off, and yet I knew my part perfectly. This is how you act when you have a dad. You are happy to see him. His projects are fun. Sometimes he lets you scratch his head or sit on his lap because you are still so little. He calls you Sport, and he jokes with you, and he doesn't mind driving you and your best friend to the Krispy Kreme donut shop at 11:00 on a Friday night because the two of you are craving "donuckles." He says things that send you and your best friend into spasmodic laughter. "A donuckle is a donuckle is a donuckle." You think he is the funniest thing in the world. Though you aren't sure if you are laughing with him or at him.

His eyes glinted, and he held his cigarette in two fingers as he scratched his cheek. I followed him out the front door and around the side of the house. There in the garage he showed me a box as tall as I was and nearly twice as long.

"What is it?" I asked.

"Look and see," he said.

I looked in the box and ran a hand inside.

"It's some kind of table," I said.

"A ping pong table," he said, pulling it out, sweat pouring from his forehead like there was a leaky pipe just under his hairline. I grabbed the box and pulled from the other end. We tugged against each other, both of us sweating until we had extracted the table.

"Damn, Richie," I said, kneeling down by the olive-green tabletop. "This is the coolest."

That night we played ping pong in the garage. And the next night and the night after that.

Tangled

We're all giddy from lack of dope on the way back from Daytona. That's a side effect of kicking that people don't tell you about. The laughing that verges on hysteria. Your back aches, your nose runs, you get a vicious case of the runs and you' re sleepless and irritable, but you can also laugh. Which is something you don't do much when you're high—not on heroin at least.

So we're cruising back to Jacksonville, AKA Cowford, in my car, the one with the backfire that goes blam, blam, blam for no reason. Timothy is searching for a radio station. He finds a country station and some southern crooner is singing. Timothy leaves the dial on the country station. Big Steve starts to sing along, "I'm so happy I could cry-y-y."

I giggle.

"What's the matter with you two?" Timothy asks. "Don't you like country music?"

Big Steve doesn't answer him. Just keeps singing in this deep voice, "What have I ever done to deserve even one of the pleasures I've known?" I'm laughing so hard tears are falling down my face in rivers.

"Y'all stop it," Timothy insists. "This is good music. What the fuck is wrong with you?"

But we don't stop, and Timothy gets more and more pissed until finally we're back in the not-so-naked city and he snaps off the radio. We pull off the interstate and drive downtown. It's gonna be impossible to cop. Any respectable junkie has gotten fixed before sunset or just after, and it's almost midnight. We cruise by the Bop Top Lounge slowly, slowly. Anyone down there knows what three white people are doing driving slowly down the street, and plenty of them signal us that they got the stuff.

"I got it, I got it," they call out and point down at the ground. But we know better. We've spent the whole day ripping people off to get this money, and we know that's exactly what they want to do to us. We circle the block slowly, eyes out for the cop cars, whispering our silent prayers that they will be somewhere else—anywhere else. We rarely speak of the possibility of getting busted. To say the words out loud would be to draw the police to you.

"Tonight's a lucky night," Timothy says.

"Yeah, I already had to do some time last night," Big Steve says. "We should be in the clear in that department."

"And Timothy and I had to deal with that pissed off chump," I say.

"We were forced to listen to country music," Big Steve says. "We paid our Karmic debt."

"Would you shut the fuck up?" Timothy says. "I mean it. I feel good luck."

We all hold our breaths, waiting to see if Timothy is right. And then we see him, the blessed Savior, Gentleman Jim in a dark suit and his old fedora. He tips his hat at us.

"Gentleman Jim, Gentleman Jim, Gentleman Jim," the three of us chant like monks. He motions us around the corner, sticks his head in the window when we get there and says, "What y'all need?"

"A half load," Timothy tells him, handing him the money. "You keep a bag for yourself." Gentleman Jim is old enough to remember sitting in the back of bus, drinking from separate water fountains, being called 'boy' —those things that my mother talked about between clenched teeth. I wonder if he sees the irony of scoring dope for the children of that race, that race that poured muriatic acid in swimming pools in order to keep blacks out.

Gentleman Jim pockets the cash and says in a loud voice for the benefit of the street lamps, "You want to take the road that way to get back to the highway." Then he whispers. "Church Street, one block down."

"Hurry, Jim, we're sick," Timothy says. As if that's going to make any difference. Gentleman Jim is the slowest guy who'll cop for you on the streets, but he's also the most honest. Gentleman Jim has never beat anyone that we know of. Never. We go park on a darkened street, wait, doze off. Then there is a rapping on the window, but instead of Gentleman Jim's handsome brown face, a face as white as the moon hangs over us, and we know that's not what we want to see. Timothy rolls down the window. We can tell it's a detective. And it doesn't pretend to be anything else.

"What y'all doin' down here?"

"Just pulled off the highway. We're traveling and we got sleepy," Timothy says. Unbelievably, the DT buys this.

"This is the wrong part of town to be taking a nap. They'll cut your throat," the detective says.

"Oh," Timothy says in alarm. He ought to win an Oscar. "Thanks, sir. We'll leave right now."

He starts the car, and we slowly pull away. We drive long enough to lose the roller behind us. And then we circle back and circle back and circle back. As usual, Gentleman Jim is taking for fuckin' ever. Finally, we see him and stop the car. Timothy starts to explain why we weren't at the meeting place, but Jim just throws a big yellow handkerchief into my lap and keeps on walking. Timothy looks in the rearview mirror. His eyes practically pop out of his head, and a little blue light goes up on the dash of the car behind us. Timothy throws the car into gear, pops the clutch and starts squealing away from the cops behind us.

"Ditch the dope, baby," he yells at me.

It's all wrapped up in this big yellow cloth, and then the car starts backfiring—blam, blam, blam. I finally get to the dope, but I can't bring myself to throw it out. My body is screaming at me not to do it, and suddenly there are shots being fired at us. Blam, blam, blam. And Big Steve grabs the dope from me and flings all the little tin foil bags out the window. Grief just rolls over me.

"They're shooting at us!" Timothy screams.

"It's okay. I threw it out," Big Steve screams back.

I don't scream anything at all; I'm silently whispering, shit, shit, shit.

Timothy pulls the car over and stops. The cops throw down like they do in the movies. "Get out of the car and reach for the stars, assholes."

We dutifully get out of the car and have our hands full of the blue night sky. The cops freak on us. They want to know where the gun is and where the dope is. Gun?

"What gun?" Timothy asks.

"We don't have a gun," I tell them.

"You were firing at us," one of them yells at me.

I drop my hands to my hips.

"That was my car backfiring," I say to them, and it's all I can do not to add "you idiots."

They rummage through the car, tossing out suntan oil and towels and cheeseburger wrappers. Then they begin to figure out that there really is no gun. And one of them says, "they threw the dope out the window." They can tell by the fact that we're not really scared that they got nothing on us. They're way too lazy to go searching the streets for a few bags of dope. One of them takes me to the side and tries to get me to talk, but I turn deaf-mute. Timothy says we didn't know they were cops, that we thought they were some dudes trying to rob us. They don't believe him, but they can't find any dope.

The next thing I know they're putting Timothy in the back of their car.

"What are you taking him for?" I ask them.

"Reckless driving," the tall one says.

I look over at Big Steve.

"That's so bogus," he says.

"Shut up, or you're going, too," the cop says. "Interfering with the law."

Big Steve and I don't say another word. We get back in the car. We drive off in one direction and the police take Timothy in the opposite direction. We're only a few blocks away when I turn the car around and head back to where we flung out the dope. I don't need to say a word. As soon as we get to the spot, Big Steve slides quickly out of the car.

His summer-green eyes shine when he jumps back in.

"I found six," he says.

"That's enough for you and me," I answer. We smile at each other and almost can't stop smiling. We start to sing, "I'm so happy I could cry-y-y."

This is one of the reasons we do this. The gamble, the risk, not knowing the outcome. This is the real drug. Tonight we threw our dice and we won. Tonight Timothy lost, but next time he'll be the one who scores. Nothing is ever the same, and in this town, sameness can be lethal. The drama is as good as the drug. We're living the movie.

Big Steve and I go to his house. We cook up all six bags and get off in the bathroom. And then we're in that place—that good place, that holy place—and we're in that place together. When we go back into his room, I climb into his bed with him, our legs intertwine, and he says, "I didn't know you liked me." Maybe he wasn't so smart, after all.

I kiss him, and he kisses me back. And I realize the dope wouldn't be any good without this kiss. I know at this moment this feeling I have now with Big Steve is more than just being high. It's also being happy. When my hands are all tangled up in his hair and his tongue, soft as a slice of peach, is deep in my mouth, I know that I am entering a different kind of love than I have known before. With Charlie, I was his "baby." But with Big Steve, I'd graduated to "girl."

The next morning when Timothy calls us from the county jail, Big Steve holds the receiver so I can hear. The first thing Timothy asks is "did y'all go back and get the bags?"

"Yes," Big Steve says.

"Did you save me any?" Timothy asks.

"No," Big Steve says. "We didn't get it all."

"Fuckers," Timothy says. I grimace when I hear him, and Big Steve looks sheepish.

We go pick up Timothy from the county jail downtown. He looks ragged, nose running, eyes red and blinking in the morning sun. He's got the jail stink all over him. When we get to my car, I hold the front seat up for him to get in the back seat. Big Steve heads around to the passenger seat up front, and that's all Timothy needs to see in order to know what happened the night before.

"I thought you were my brother, man," Timothy says to Big Steve.

"It was meant to be, man," Big Steve tells him.

"You coming or what?" I ask Timothy.

He gives me a pitiful, betrayed look and then says, "We better get to work if we're gonna get high today."

Timothy gets in the back seat and leans his head between me and Big Steve as I drive away from the cop station, and drive along the sluggish blue-brown river. My car goes blam, blam, blam.

A Lovely Place

Timothy, Big Steve and I sat on a bus in San Diego, rolling toward Ocean Beach. My first day in California, and already I was being exposed to a new set of rules. The bus rumbled through sharp, crystalline sunlight.

"You lowlife bastards," I said. We occupied the back seats that face each other. No one else was back there except for this Chinese-looking chick in way-high platform shoes across the aisle from me. "I oughta leave both of you here. That dope was mine just as much as it was yours."

Timothy and Big Steve were glassy-eyed, scratching their red faces.

"Sneaking into the men's bathroom of a laundromat. Motherfuckers."

Big Steve leaned over, his hot breath oozing over his tongue.

"I'm sorry, girl. I promise we'll get you some as soon as we get to Ocean Beach. There wasn't enough for all three of us," he said in a sandpaper voice. His minuscule pupils focused on my forehead. I wanted to punch him.

"The hell there wasn't," I hissed. "Look at you greasy sons of bitches. Greasy!"

The woman was listening to us, but I didn't care. I could have kicked both of their sorry asses, placed my seven and a half all the way up their rectums. They were worse than Charlie with his damn g-shots.

"Everything is three way," I said. "Everything! That money is just as much mine as anyone else's."

"Sorry, Trish," Big Steve said, but he didn't mean it.

I settled back with my arms crossed, thinking, they're going to pay for this treachery one way or another. I just hadn't figured out how. And since I'd never been to California before, I was dependent on them for the time being. Back at home, I owned the car and that gave me the power. Here, I had nothing except the money we had stolen from someone's checking account—this kid who gave us a check from his Mom. He told his mom he needed to get his transmission fixed, but he really thought he was buying some old ragweed that Big Steve had. We changed the check amount from 250 dollars to 2500. It was a bigger rip off than we'd done before, and for a while, we'd felt like jet set dopers. We were Keith Richards et al, but this betrayal—well, now I knew where I stood. I wasn't even holding the money. It wouldn't have done me any good if I were because I had no idea how to cop on this coast. I stared out the window—everything was alien to me, even the dusty looking flowers that peppered the brown yards. I might as well have traveled to another planet.

Then sound disappeared the way it does sometimes when something is about to change. I turned my head and stared right into the black eyes of the Asian woman. She gave me a slight smile, and it felt like my thoughts were transmitting right into her head.

She leaned over and said, "Hey, what did they do? Get off without you?"

"Yeah," I said.

"I got some stuff," she said. "Back at my place. Come on over. I'll sell you a quarter spoon."

I'd heard about earthquakes in California, and I could tell that something had slipped in that moment.

"Who are you?" I asked.

"I'm Mary," she said. When she smiled, her nose crinkled.

"I'm Trish," I told her. Then I looked over at the boys.

"We're going over to Mary's crib," I said. "And you fuckers are gonna watch while I get off. Instant Karma."

And everything was all right once again.

Mary lived in an apartment complex just north of the Mexican border. She had three kids—a girl six, a boy about four and a two-and-half-year-old girl. Beautiful children, but filthy and the littlest one stunk from dirty diapers. The six year old, Justina, looked nothing like Mary, except for her almond eyes. She was blond and looked Scandinavian. Mary said they each had a different father. But Mary wasn't a hooker. She wanted us to know that. She was a dealer.

The apartment was a small two-bedroom place with linoleum floors and turquoise Naugahyde furniture that Mary said had been supplied by the California welfare department. Crayon lines of blue, purple and yellow decorated the hallway; children's toys were scattered everywhere. These are my babies, Mary said, kissing the littlest one. But then admitted she hadn't seen much of them since she went to jail for a year shortly after the last one was born.

On a shelf she had a bunch of knickknacks—Chinese dolls from her mother, and Mexican pottery from her paternal grandfather, and a collection of handcuffs that she got from God knows where.

"I'm one big melting pot," she said, sticking a lollipop in the littlest kid's mouth.

The first night we were there, six-year-old Justina crawled into my lap and played with my hair. Her almond eyes locked onto mine and she asked if I would take her to the zoo.

"One of these days," I answered.

After Mary and I got off, we sat outside in metal chairs. The night air was chilly, which surprised me since it was already May. In Florida it would be warm now. An orangish haze coated the sky so the stars were hardly visible.

Mary pointed down to the lighted area below us.

"I'll take you to Tijuana tomorrow," she said. "I have to go anyway. You can cop maybe an ounce of dope with the money you got."

"You speak Spanish?" I asked.

"Si," she said and turned to me with a smile. How could we possibly have gotten so lucky, I wondered. We lived our lives so fatefully, falling into situations, meeting people on buses. There was no other way my life could have gone than the way it was going. And that was the thrill of it—we didn't have to plan a thing. We stood in the middle of traffic and waited to see what would hit us next.

"The dope from Tijuana is so good, Chiquita," Mary said and scratched her face. "Better than the best cock."

The next day Mary and I were back in Mary's bedroom with a quarter spoon of dope, and my veins were acting up. As soon as I went after one, it sank down out of sight as if it was scared and trying to hide from me. The younger kids were outside the bedroom door, crying.

"Shut up!" Mary screamed at them. She finally managed to puncture a hole in my arm and ease the drug into my vein. I sat back. The whole room loosened. I watched Mary tie the leg from a pair of panty hose around her upper arm, watched her stick a needle into a scarred piece of vein, shoot the blackish water in and then saw her face go slack and soft as a roll of wet toilet paper. As Mary cleaned out the needle, she squirted the bloody water into the back of her throat instead of onto the wall or on the inside of her jeans cuff the way we always did. I thought of a snake that swallows its own tail.

"This is how we do it in California," she said.

"Why?" I asked.

She shrugged. "You don't want to waste any dope, do you?"

"Certainly not," I said. I filled my needle with water which turned pale pink and then squirted it into the back of my throat.

Neither of us heard the kids crying outside the door anymore. Children didn't exist in the place where we had gone.

Hot Town

Big Steve, Timothy and I wandered around the blistering market streets of Tijuana. Sunlight plastered the walls, the sidewalks, the ground.

"Muy caliente," we muttered to each other, very hot. The street was crowded with tourists and sailors. We dove into shops for the shade and found ourselves surrounded by leather. The smell made me groggy.

"Look at this coat," I said to Big Steve, my fingers on the sleeve of a dark suede car coat. "It's gorgeous."

A Mexican woman breathed against my shoulder.

"Quanto es?" I asked her slowly, proud of these few words. Her black eyes met mine.

"Vente," she answered, tossing the price in the air like a tennis ball.

"Did she say twenty?" I asked Big Steve. He shrugged. I showed the woman a twenty dollar bill. She slipped it out of my fingers and handed me the coat.

We walked back outside, slap into a wall of heat. Timothy stood there as if the heat was holding him up like a pair of giant hands. I could see the sweat as it evaporated from the skin of his temples. I held up my coat for him to see.

"What the fuck did you get a coat for?" he wanted to know.

"It gets chilly here at night," I said. "Besides it was only twenty bucks. I'll never find another coat like this as long as I live. At least a coat is something that you'll have, something you can use."

An old black Chevrolet churned by, silver exhaust reaching out like a scalding tongue to touch our legs. Standing there in the heat in the middle of the street surrounded by whirling words that I didn't understand, under a pale heartless sky, I felt as if a shell had cracked open, as if I could see us all clearly in this one instance—how doomed and pathetic we were, thinking we were some kind of romantic outlaws, when we were just bourgeois trash. Before I knew it, I was yelling at Timothy.

"It's not just cramming the money into a needle every day. It's not just a complete waste of our fucking lives. What the hell is wrong with you? You just want to cook it up, don't you? And then it's gone and there's nothing. Not a goddamn thing." I looked at Big Steve, and I looked at Timothy, and they stared off into space like characters in a movie, like they couldn't hear a word I'd said, but they knew I spoke the gospel right then.

Then Timothy said, "You're just hungry. Let's get some tacos."

The shell snapped shut over my mind, and my anger vanished like the smell of the exhaust. I could stuff it down. I could live this life. Hell, I chose it. Or did it choose me? I wasn't sure anymore.

I followed Timothy to a small table that looked like some kid's lemonade stand. A barefooted, sharp-eyed boy told us the tacos cost two pesos. So I gave him two quarters which he pocketed quickly before handing over a soft taco wrapped around shredded beef. I bit into it—hot, dry and exquisitely delicious.

"This sure as hell ain't Taco Bell," I said. We ate about five or six of them and then we wandered into another little stall along the market. An old man with long black braids sat behind a table full of turquoise jewelry—rings, bracelets, earrings. Some of the stones were blue, others green and some had red blotches in them.

"Blood turquoise," Big Steve said, pointing to the red. Then he picked up a silver ring with a green triangle-shaped stone. He put it on my finger. His dark blond hair fell across his forehead. His eyes were the same color as the stone.

"How much?" he asked the old man.

"Twenty-five dollars American, por favor," the old man said. Big Steve pulled out his wallet and handed over the money.

"Jesus Christ," Timothy said. "Are you guys gonna spend it all before Mary comes back? What the hell are you thinking?"

I looked down at the ring. It was lovely.

"Thanks, baby," I said to Big Steve.

"Aw, come on," Timothy said, rolling his eyes. "Thanks, baby?"

When we met Mary back at the corner by a bar called The Blue Note, she said that I could come with her but they'd have to wait. Mary's jiggled the car keys in her hand, a look of pure business on her face. She ought to be running corporations, I thought.

Big Steve squeezed my hand, his mustache brushed against my cheek, Timothy gave me a long look and told me to be careful, and then I took off with Mary into the blinding light of Tijuana.

Burn, Burn, Burn

"You'll like Rudolfo," Mary said. "He's very quiet and mysterious."

"It's like being inside a kiln, this car," I said. It was an old Pontiac she'd borrowed from one of her neighbors.

"I got you some rubbers from the farmacia," Mary said and handed me a small package of unlubricated condoms. We were at a stoplight, but a taxi pulled around her and ran it. I was glad she was driving instead of me. A horn blared at us. I hung my arm out the window. The car's air conditioner was useless.

"Where are we going?" I asked.

"To La Mesa," she answered. "It's like a suburb but not really. More of a ghetto or a barrio."

We drove away from the tourist area of Tijuana into a vast desert of apartment buildings, sand-colored buildings, pink buildings, lopsided turquoise and red brick houses with sullen-eyed children hanging from rickety wooden porches, watching us drive by.

"I have to go a roundabout way to make sure the federales aren't following," she said. Her black hair gleamed like wet paint in the sun. I was wearing a peasant blouse that had become heavy with my sweat. I stared into the side view mirror. My eyes looked like the eyes of a stranger watching me sadly. It had been hours since I'd had any dope.

We turned down a narrow street. On one side the houses were hidden by thick green foliage. On the other side, white and brown apartments pushed against the road. A small pig ran out from under a bush, and Mary had to hit the brakes in order not to obliterate it.

"Chinga tu madre," she said. Then she pulled down a narrow drive into a tunnel of jungle. Branches made high screeching noises like screams against the car.

Inside the apartment, everything becomes sharp and distinct—the green walls, the oval rug, the coffee table, the two mismatched couches and the three young men sitting one on each couch and another in a wooden chair.

"Hey, amigos," Mary says with a broad smile. They smile back at us. They wear button down shirts and slacks and look like they're dressed up for church.

"Esta es Trish de Florida," she says, but she says "Treesh" and I like the way it swims out of her mouth like a goldfish. Then she turns to me. "These are Rudolfo's brothers and his cousin."

"Sit, mamacitas," one of them says, moving over to give us room on one of the couches. We sit down. It's cooler in the room, and a rotating fan takes turns blowing on us.

"Mamacita means little mama," Mary tells me. "It's a compliment."

Mary starts spewing Mexican at them, and they listen and laugh. They are talking about me, I can tell that much. Then the tallest one says to me, "Speak to us, Trish de Florida." So right then I know Mary has been telling them about my southern accent, which she can't get over.

"La cerveza is muy buen," I say to them, thinking that my accent will disappear in their language. They laugh and slap their thighs. I feel like I'm twelve years old. Like an idiot. I smile politely, feeling like a monkey on a leash and wondering where the hell is this Rudolfo guy, but by now I know better than to ask. Being a junkie has taught me patience. You slide into another time zone when you're waiting for heroin; you breathe slowly; you become the Buddha.

One of the brothers passes a milk jug to me. I look inside. Water?

"It's tequila," Mary says, and her dark eyebrows shift just a little. "They want you to have some."

I don't like alcohol, but I take a sip. It sears my esophagus all the way down to my gut.

"Dear God," I say, choking and blinking back tears. They laugh uproariously.

A man enters.

"Rudolfo," Mary says. The door closes behind him. He comes over to me and holds out a slender hand. I take his hand as his eyes slither over me. It occurs to me at this particular moment, they could kill me and no one would ever know. No one would ever find my body.

"Come with me," Rudolfo says. Mary sits back down, and I follow him into another room. I wish Mary would come, too, but I'm not making the rules here.

He closes the door. We are in a bedroom. Dark green curtains cloak the window. There is no rug on the linoleum floor. A color TV sits on a stand in the corner. Suddenly I notice he isn't as tall as I thought he was. His skin is light mocha, and the light from a lamp on the dresser makes a silver glow on his straight, black hair. His features are so finely etched it looks as though someone has carved out the fat underneath the skin with a scalpel.

"Do you have a rubber?" he asks.

I reach into my purse and open the package. I pull out a long, skinny rubber and hand it to him.

"Good," he says. A set of scales sits on the dresser and he pulls a large baggie with two tinfoil packets from the top drawer.

"This is only twelve hundred," he says.

"That's all it's supposed to be," I tell him.

"Fourteen," he says.

"Bullshit."

He's staring at me with eyes as hard as that emerald on his finger. I decide not to say anything, but I look away as if I'm suddenly bored.

"You need this dope, gringa," he says.

"No, I do not," I tell him, thinking that Big Steve and Timothy are going to have a raging fit if I come back empty-handed. But now I am pretty sure no one is going to kill me, and the relief makes me want to laugh. I don't. Rudolfo smiles, not at me, but at himself.

"Okay, mamacita," he says dumping grains of dark brown dope from the tinfoil onto the scales. "I'll give you twenty-seven grams."

Not quite as much as we expected, but enough. Certainly enough. I nod my head and then watch carefully as he pushes the little silver bar on the scale to 27. He looks at me, eyebrows arched, and I touch the dope with my little finger. I take a quick taste—bitter. Good enough. Certainly good enough. I nod again, and he takes a small spoon and dumps the dope into the rubber where it falls down into the tip. He ties the rubber around the ball at the end. And then manages to fold it several times over.

"There," he says, handing it to me. "Very secure."

I feel the weight of it in my hand. Never have I had so much dope in my hand before. A giddiness attacks me. I feel an absurd adoration of this strange man. He has not killed me. Instead he has given me this dark orgasm.

I go into the bathroom and push the rubber as far into my vagina as it will go. Mary says it's the safest way. And no one at the border will check me unless I do something suspicious.

When I come out of the bedroom, Mary is gone. One of the brothers hands me the keys to the Pontiac.

Don't Touch My Bags

I headed down the street in the Pontiac; some little kids jumped and laughed and pretended to be run over. Darkness flowed over the landscape, and I wished I had understood exactly what Rudolfo's brothers were trying to tell me. Mary had gone off with Rudolfo's cousin, that much was clear. I did not need to wait for her, they said. I did not dare wait for her. But where was the border? Both of them talking to me at once. Go this way, turn that way. Most of it in Spanish.

At the corner I knew I needed to turn left. That much I was sure of. I could tell by the direction of the darkness that left would take me north. And north was where I wanted to go. I looked down at the gas gauge. Enough? I wasn't sure. Street lights in La Mesa were rare diamonds. Where's the North Star, I wondered. The whole sky became black, and it was only by feel that I was sure that the sun set that way—to my left. I drove blindly, stopping, slowing down. Turn here? I hit a dead end. Just houses, and many of them dark. Didn't they have electricity? Shit. I turned around.

At the corner I wondered, do I go left or right? I tried to back track and start over again, but nothing was recognizable.

I wondered about Big Steve and Timothy. If they were waiting for me, I'd never find them. I couldn't figure out why Mary left me. Maybe she snitched me out to the border patrol. The only way I'd find out was if they searched me. Of course, I might never find the border.

I continued to drive through Tijuana, afraid to stop and ask somebody the way to the border. Was I going in circles or heading in the wrong direction? One time when I was about fifteen, I went scuba diving with Shannon and her parents. Underwater it was impossible to tell which way you were going. That's how I felt in Tijuana. I was running out of air.

I came out on a road, and the houses were gone. I stopped at an intersection and put my head down on the steering wheel and cried bitter stinging tears. Then that voice came to me—my guardian angel or private demon, I didn't know what. It said: "Right."

So I turned right and after a few miles, I arrived at the edge of the tourist district. Some drunk sailors stumbled out of a bar and fell into a rental car. I followed them. The border was only a few minutes away, stretching out like a big toll booth all lit up. The border guards would wonder what a woman was doing in Tijuana by herself and why she was coming back at night. I wondered if I should wait and go back tomorrow, but inside me this pitchfork jabbed my brain, telling me to get back to Mary's, get back to Big Steve, get back to a set of works.

I slowed down as I approached the border. I was going through no matter what. The drunk sailors in the rental car in front of me swerved over the lane. I felt as if I was watching some sort of surreal cartoon. The rental car lurched forward and seemed to pounce on the car next to it. The metal frames of the two cars groaned as they crumpled and twisted in the force of the crash.

As I drove past, one of the drunk sailors got out of the rental car, his head bleeding. I kept driving and when I got to the border patrol, my hands shook as I pulled out my driver's license.

"The wreck," I said to the customs man, my eyes watery with dope need.

"Did you see the wreck?" My voice trembled. The customs man patted me on the hand as he returned my license.

"Yeah. We'll get an ambulance. You go on and take it easy," he said.

"Thank you, " I whispered. "Thank you."

When I got to Mary's apartment, Big Steve looked up at me from the couch where he sat. Justina, Mary's little girl, was on Big Steve's lap. Timothy lay on the floor, a pillow under his head. The television was on. The other kids were asleep on the floor.

“Where’s Momma?” Justina asked.

“I don’t know,” I answered. Justina’s eyes looked at me blankly, and then she turned back to the television. Clearly, Mary’s disappearance was not a surprise to her.

“I was lost,” I said to Big Steve.

Big Steve told the little girl to go to bed, then he came over and put his arms around me. I didn’t realize until that moment how badly I was shaking.

“Did you get it?” Timothy asked.

That night I lay next to Big Steve in Mary’s bed. We’d shot a lot of dope, so much that sleep was impossible. Instead delirium surrounded us. I kept following streets that led nowhere and rousing from these dreams with a start.

“Easy, girl,” Big Steve would say, and then he’d say something nonsensical, something crazy like, “The cats won’t hurt you.”

All night it went like that—me driving through dark streets, unable to read the signs or understand the people who stopped to give me directions. I was grateful when the shades of Mary’s windows were tinged with light. I didn’t even want a wake-up shot right away.

I went into the living room and found Mary asleep on the couch. Her mouth hung open. Her lips had no color to them. I stared at her for a long time. I wanted to wake her up and ask her why she had left me, but I figured she probably wouldn’t even know. Hell, she left her own kids all the time. Why should she worry about me? I had to remind myself once again that friendship had no meaning, and that love just meant you had someone to hold your arm while you got off. We thought this loveless was worth it for the sublime joy of puncturing our veins and ripping into whatever had put us together in the first place.

We got a flight back to Florida that afternoon.

I'll Fly Away

Back home. We checked into a cheap motel and had to sell some dope fast because we were almost out of cash. The three of us headed over to the methadone clinic which had once again been moved. No one wants a bunch of junkies skulking around their neighborhood. The clinic was now in the depths of downtown in a dilapidated brick building that was sure to be condemned any moment. We parked across the street and scanned the morning crowd for a familiar face. Well, all the faces were familiar, but some would be friendlier than others. News of our caper must have gotten around. Hungry, jealous eyes watched us. And then I noticed Jasper Collins leaning against the building.

"When did he get on the program?" I wondered aloud.

Jasper saw me and wandered over. He rested his arms inside the window.

"You on this poison?" I asked him.

"Nah, just looking to cop," Jasper said. "Hey, I heard you guys went to California. Bring back anything good?"

"Yeah, we got some dope for sale," Big Steve said. "Go ask Timothy."

Jasper's eyes sparkled. Behind him I could see Timothy canvassing the junkies waiting for their doses.

"I know some guys that'll buy all you got," Jasper said, shifting his weight back and forth in excitement. "Where can I find you later?"

"We're at the Red Court on the Westside," I told him. "Room 217. But don't bring anybody with you, Jasper. Come by yourself."

"Shit, do I look stupid?" he said.

"Sometimes," I answered. Jasper cut his eyes at me. Jasper had cheated off my tests and copied my homework whenever possible in high school, so being stupid was a sore spot for him. But he could usually make me laugh, which was a kind of smartness.

"All right, see you later," Jasper said and headed over to Timothy.

A mutt walked up to Timothy and started sniffing him in the crotch which made me and Big Steve burst out laughing. Timothy waved the dog away. The dog had sweet, yearning dog eyes and a shiny brown coat though he was hungry, no doubt about it.

"Hey, whose dog is that?" Big Steve called out to one of the methadone regulars.

"Don't nobody own that dog," she answered. "It's been coming around here for days." She flicked her cigarette butt down on the ground, and the dog lunged for it.

Big Steve and I looked at each other, and in a minute we had the car door open. The dog crawled in the back seat where he foraged for old french fries. Timothy sold a little bit of the dope, and we headed back to the motel with Timothy and the dog in the back seat.

"Y'all gonna keep this damn dog?" he asked.

"He already has a name," I said. "We're calling him Boner." I was imagining Big Steve and me living in a little house with a yard paid for with the profits from our dope sales. Then I thought maybe we'd get on the methadone. Or maybe we'd kick outright. Get jobs. Maybe I could work in a night club. Have a house and Boner. It all seemed possible. Big Steve and I grinned at each other.

In revenge, Timothy went and got Cynthia, his ex-wife, and brought her to the motel where we were staying. She had long red hair and was slightly cross-eyed. Startlingly beautiful, she was incensed about my very existence. Big Steve got this stupid slack-jawed look on his face whenever her back was turned, and then I would crack up. She wanted to know why I was always laughing.

We're all in the motel room back in Jacksonville, the dope on the dresser where Timothy has started bagging it up for sale. He has already mixed it with some cut. Our plan is to make a hundred to two hundred percent profit and then go back to California for more "doojie"—which I cannot for the life of me tell you how to spell. Very entrepreneurish, we think. Little squares of tinfoil sit by the larger baggie, and Timothy methodically puts a little dollop of dope into the middle of a square and folds it up. This is how dope is sold in Jacksonville, not in balloons like California.

Timothy has bought a gun and keeps it in the drawer. I don't like having guns around, but I know about this place. This town has a larcenous heart like Charlie always said. It's the navy bases. Too much easy money.

Boner is lying between the beds, licking hamburger wrappers. We've decided that he likes Burger King burgers best of all, and we gave him three whopper juniors and a milkshake for breakfast that day.

Big Steve and I lie on one of the beds. Some insipid soap opera is on. Cynthia loves "General Hospital," so Big Steve and I start imitating everything the characters say, Oh, Luke! Oh, Laura! I love you! until she screams at us to just shut up, just shut up. We throw the covers over our heads and laugh. Then his hands are sliding up and down the white slip that I am wearing and we're in that dopey kind of place, not so high that we can't laugh and have fun but not hurting. It's a good place. We forget about Timothy and Cynthia. His mouth finds mine. I feel the warmth of his body, the landscape of his legs, and the soft insistent pressure of his fingers.

Bang! Bang!

"Open up the fuckin' door. Police!"

Big Steve tumbles out of the bed and looks through a crack in the curtains.

"Those aren't cops, man," he says.

"Who the fuck are they?" Timothy asks.

"They look like bikers, and they got guns," Big Steve says.

Someone starts kicking in the door and making damn good headway.

Big Steve lies down between the beds. He grabs the phone and dials the motel operator.

"We're being robbed," he tells her. "Call the police."

I go into the bathroom and stand in the shower. Timothy pulls out his gun, which is just a .22, but it's all we got. The door caves in. I can hear wood splinter and crack. Timothy comes into the bathroom with me and points his gun at them through the doorway. Cynthia stands up and says, "I'm not with them. Let me out of here."

She walks past the bikers and goes outside. Timothy tosses a wad of tinfoil into the toilet and flushes. He still has the baggie of dope in his hand.

"Where's the dope, motherfuckers?" one of the guys screams at him. "Give it to us, or we'll kill you."

"I'll kick your motherfucking ass!" somebody says. And it sounds like Big Steve is taking a bad beating. I can't ever imagine him fighting even being as big as he is. I'm actually wishing the cops would come in a hurry.

"Stop it, you motherfucker, or I'll blow your head off," Timothy yells at the guy. The sounds stop. "Go on. Get out of the fucking door."

"Are you all right, man?" Timothy yells out to Big Steve.

"Yeah," Big Steve answers.

"You fucking junkies," one of the other guys yells at us. "You fucking scum."

"Don't shoot," I whisper to Timothy. I'm thinking about how we'll all go to prison for murder if somebody dies. I can't figure out which is worse—to have them kill us or to kill them and spend the rest of our lives in prison.

"I'm sorry, man. I didn't know they were gonna rob you," a voice says. It's Jasper. And I was the genius who told him where we were staying.

Then one of the other guys says, "Shit. The cops are here, man."

Timothy looks at me. I hold out my hand. He gives me the gun, and then he turns around, drops the baggie of heroin into the toilet, and flushes. It's all I can do not to shoot him.

I hear footsteps, those big-daddy cop voices, saying, "Now, what's going on here?"

The whole time I'm standing behind the shower curtain, and Boner is standing in the bathtub next to me. Timothy goes into the room to talk to the cops.

When one of the cops comes in the bathroom, Boner growls at him, and he turns around and says, "Nobody in there. Just a dog." I've become invisible. I look down at that gorgeous, intelligent dog and feel glad that someone, at least, is on my side.

Finally, the cops take the other guys away.

I wait a few minutes before I come out of the shower. I go into the room. Cynthia is sitting in the chair by the window. Jasper is collapsed on the floor, holding his nose. Blood flows from it like a faucet.

Timothy and Big Steve and I look at each other. Big Steve has a yellow and blue bruise on his face where the guy kicked him.

"Where's the dope?" Big Steve asks.

"It's gone," Timothy says.

"Fuck," Big Steve says.

"I didn't want to go to prison," Timothy says. Big Steve looks down at the floor. Timothy doesn't move. Cynthia is mercifully silent.

"I didn't know they were going to rob you guys, I swear," Jasper says. His voice sounds clogged with blood.

"Shut the fuck up," Timothy yells at him.

Then I do the only thing that makes the situation bearable. I pull seven small tin foil bags of heroin out of my underpants.

"You left these," I say to Timothy.

We decided to drive my car back to California. We went to Big Steve's mom's house to ask her to keep Boner. Big Steve's mom stood on her doorstep and glared out at me. I looked away, but she came down towards the car and started yelling at me.

"Leave her alone, Mom," Big Steve said.

"Doesn't she have any self-respect?" she yelled at him, spitting fury.

I wondered what had gotten her all wound up on me, but I knew that I had a way of making mothers hate me. Who would want to blame their own child when someone else's child was so conveniently making the same mistakes?

Big Steve tried to pull her away from the car. Boner sat down and watched the action with the cool temperament I had come to admire.

"Why don't you stay away from my son?" his mother screamed at me.

I felt bad. I knew that if I were her, I would hate me, too. Finally, she turned around and headed back into the house.

"Go on, Boner," Big Steve said. Boner took one last look at us, and then went inside after her.

Timothy and I took turns driving. The songs on the radio that year were especially egregious—"How long has this been going on?" "Wildfire," "Havin' my Baby." We knew them all by heart. Cynthia was with us and she tried to scathe me with her eyeballs every time "How long has this been going on?" came on.

"Why don't you get over it?" I asked her, but she wouldn't answer me. Sometimes under her breath, she'd call me a slut. If I hadn't been feeling so awful, I'd have laughed.

Timothy and I had a puke bag that we passed back and forth between us. Big Steve didn't have the jones nearly as bad as we did. It was his body size or that Zen shit he studied in prison. Of course, we all had terrible gas and the car stank like rotten eggs.

We drove through all these little towns, but we had no way to get drugs. We drove straight through the first night: Tallahassee, Pensacola, Mobile, New Orleans. It was dawn as we crossed the Mississippi. Good morning, America. How the hell are you?

The second day lasted about four-thousand hours. This was Texas, big and sometimes bleakly beautiful. I was mesmerized by the accumulation of images—the run-down trailer park clothesline yard America and the pristine lawn locked in their house with the 2-car garage America. There was the America I had seen in the movies and the America I was now seeing with my eyes. There was a brown America and a green America and then the solid gray of the cities. I tried to imagine the pioneers, wondering how they managed to get across all this dirt, all these rocks, these scrubby plants, these gorges. Were their lives as miserable as ours now? But no matter how long it took them to get across, no matter how hungry or tired or thirsty they must have been, they still had their souls. My soul, on the other hand, was depleted. It was just a flickering candle in a hurricane, and my heart was like the Texas sky—empty as far as the eye could see.

Outside El Paso the sunset was dragon's breath red, and then night slipped a cover over the landscape. We kept going, but we were stuck in the middle of this big indecipherable continent. If I could have set off an atomic bomb right then, I would've.

"We can sleep out here," Timothy said. We got out of the car with blankets and tried to find a soft place on the ground to sleep. Big Steve wouldn't lie down near me. When he was dope sick, his heart turned to ice. The air outside was freezing. I had never been so miserable in my life. Everything ached. Every bone, every piece of skin. My muscles jerked and spasmed like a puppet. Even my blood hurt. I finally stood up.

"Fuck this," I told the others. I took the keys from Timothy and headed for the car.

"Where are you going?" Timothy wanted to know.

"I saw a motel back there about three or four miles."

"She is so spoiled," Cynthia said. Her constant refrain through the whole trip.

"We can't spare the money, Trish," Timothy said.

"Yes, we can," I told him. "I'm going. You guys want me to pick you up in the morning?"

They all got up and trundled after me. This one time they were all grateful in their frozen little hearts that I was "so spoiled."

In the motel room, Big Steve and Cynthia fell asleep on the two beds. Timothy and I lay next to them, unable to shut our eyes or to still our tortured bodies. Finally, I got up, went into the bathroom and drew a hot bath. And for about 20 blessed minutes, the pain went away. The water nursed me like a loving mama. I got out, slipped on a T-shirt and told Timothy what I'd found—relief in the water.

"Really?" he asked. Then gratefully he got up and took a long hot bath.

I never did get any sleep that night. In the morning I put on my bathing suit and went out into the pool. The water there helped, too. This was the only thing, the only relief. At my mom's apartment there was a swimming pool. My mom and I used to swim together all the time. My mother would do these long-armed laps. I'd go underwater, the whole length in one breath. When I was little, my mother, who was a lifeguard when she was a teenager, practiced her life-saving skills on me. She'd crook her arm gently around my neck and pull me as I floated on my back to the edge of the pool. I knew that's what she wished she could do now.

As we got back into the car to continue our journey, I wondered what my mother was doing, if she was glad I was gone, or if she was insane enough to miss me. I wondered if she was playing her piano or reading a book or staring out at the oak trees or laughing on the phone with a friend. My mother's laughter was like a waterfall.

In Arizona the road spilled like an endless trail of oil across the desert, which was nothing like I thought it would be. I guess I expected "Lawrence of Arabia"—huge golden sand dunes and all that—but this desert was a brownish green stubble of round little cactus plants and shrubs, long yellow grasses, pebbles and telephone poles sprouting out of the ground. Just out of arm's reach, mountains rose and then fell. One particularly smooth silhouette against a sky so blue you could drink it took the shape of a woman, upturned nose, and the breasts, belly, hips sloping down to nothing. It made me think of a dead woman. It made me think of myself.

Your Cheatin' Heart

The occasional screwdriver that my step-father Richie drinks at parties turns into an everyday event. One morning I come down the stairs into the kitchen to find he is drinking vodka straight out of the bottle.

Mother has rehearsal for the symphony. As usual I am going with her. Richie, oddly enough, is sober as Mom and I head out the door. I'm wearing my ripped jeans and carrying a book to read. *Great Expectations*. Richie's cigarette smoke shrouds his eyes as he walks with us to the door. My mother smiles at him. She believes that Richie's drinking was just a temporary thing. She wears black pants and a black sweater and her Estée Lauder perfume floats carelessly around her.

I suddenly look up at Richie as if he's done something strange, but he's just plain old crinkly-around-the-eyes Richie. Then it happens. I can't seem to hear anything for a moment except a cool voice right up against my ear, and it says, "Have a good time, Richie."

I have never heard it so strong before. I have never even imagined what I know in this moment to be true.

That night we go to the rehearsal. I hear the familiar hum and groan of instruments being tuned.

"Mom, I'm sick," I tell her. I have no control over this lie.

She rolls her eyes.

"Why didn't you say something earlier?" she asks, peevish. Worry makes her irritated.

"I think I'm going to throw up," I say. "I have to go home."

"You do look flushed," she says. And then with sudden guilt for her earlier irritation, she tells the conductor she has to leave.

"What about the rehearsal?" he asks. She is the solo pianist.

"I'll be right back," she says, and turns to go with me following her, trying to look as desperately ill as I possibly can.

In the car she wants to know if my stomach hurts and how bad is it and does she need to pull off to the side of the road.

"Just get me home," I say. And she does. We both recognize the beat-up looking Falcon in front of the house. It belongs to one of Richie's high school chorus students, my baby-sitter, a scabby-skinned girl who called us up one time to joyfully announce that someone killed Martin Luther King, Jr. My mother refused to let her baby-sit for me after that.

My mother and I walk up to the door. She slides the key into the lock and swings the door open. Even from where I am on the porch, I can see that the living room lights are dim. Then my mother charges inside and she's pursuing the baby-sitter up the stairs, screaming, "Get out of my house. Get the hell out of here!"

The baby-sitter's shoes lie on the floor of the living room like shells, and Richie sits regally on the love seat with a drink in his hand. He calmly takes a sip as the girl comes running back down the steps and out the door. My mother finds the shoes and throws them outside at the girl standing on the sidewalk. Richie finishes his drink, looks at me, and shrugs his shoulders. I go upstairs to my room.

Summer arrives likes a black hole. My mom and Richie are still together, but none of us has much to say to each other. One night when mother is asleep, I get up and go downstairs for some water. Richie is in the kitchen, drinking Beefeater's gin. I ignore him as I pour a glass of cold water from the plastic pitcher in the refrigerator.

"It's not my fault," he says.

I don't answer him. I take my glass of water and start back up the stairs, but Richie follows me.

He clutches my hand, which is on the newel post. I glare at him but he holds on. "You know she slept with other men. That's why your father left her. Before we were married, she took back her key from me. She's not faithful."

I am only fourteen years old. I may be precocious in some ways, but I don't understand the world of adults. Later when

I'm an adult myself, I will realize two things: women have needs and sometimes jealous men lie. But right now I feel as if I am standing naked. My skin grows tight around my neck. And his hand feels like a large snail on mine. I pull away from him. I don't say a word. I go upstairs, and I lock the chain lock across my door. Then I lie down and close my eyes.

I know what having a father means in other families. I have seen it—both the bad and the good. It means you get smacked with a belt if you say a cuss word. It means you can't play the television too loud on Saturday mornings or you'll get into big undefined trouble. But it also means that you have cookouts, you go camping, you get fireworks on the fourth of July. Sometimes it means that you're rich and you have a horse or a beach house. You go on family vacations if you have a father. And you don't get in trouble at school. You don't scrawl cuss words on your desk in the sixth grade. You don't steal candy from the Minit Market across the street from school.

Now I know something else: Step-fathers don't count, not if they turn into alcoholics right before your eyes.

California Girls

We hit the state line—Welcome to California. The sun hammered down on us like a mallet. We passed mountains as blue as the ocean. Sitting in the passenger side, I pulled strands of hair in front of my eyes like blinds. I stared fascinated as the strands turned into prism catching the sunlight. Then a cramping seized my gut, and I wished we were near a bathroom.

"Where the fuck is everybody going?" Timothy asked, looking at the traffic converging on the interstate.

"To San Diego," I answered.

"For a fix," Big Steve added.

Then it turned into a race, and all the other cars were at once rivals and comrades.

Our first night back in San D., we headed straight over to Mary's. We knocked on the door and stood there, all four of us. The little girl, Justina, opened the door. I gave her a hug and walked inside. Mary was on a big nod, sitting in an old chair in the corner of the room. The television blaring. Her other kids were nowhere to be seen.

"Hey, mamacita," I said. "We back."

Mary looked up at me, and scratched her nose.

"Yeah, and we're sick as shit," Timothy said. "Got any dope you can sell us?"

"Oh God," Cynthia said. I turned around and saw her staring into the kitchen.

Justina had gone back to watching television. I walked over to where Cynthia was standing. The refrigerator door was open and food was spilled all over—ketchup, mustard, mayonnaise, broken eggs, milk, gnawed off pieces of bread. Mary must have gotten food stamps while we were gone.

"Justina, what happened in here?" I called out to the little girl.

"The kids got hungry," she said. "They ate some bread, and I put them to bed."

"Maybe you ought to clean that up," I told Cynthia. She looked at me with so much hatred that I couldn't help laughing. "Shit. I'll do it, Cyn. Just let me get off first. I feel like I'm gonna puke again."

Mary slowly, ever so slowly, rummaged through drawers and found her dope. Timothy and I got off first. Our noses were running and we could hardly stand still while the dope bubbled in the cooker. I held my arm while Mary found a vein down on my wrist. She sent that dark dope into my blood tunnels, and it ran like a zipper from my arm to the top of my head and down to the soles of my feet.

"Lord have mercy," I whispered. "Thank you. Thank you, God."

That night, Mary let me and Steve have her bed. Steve and I were nice to each other for the first time since we lost the dope. I didn't want to think about what that said about our relationship, but it was pretty obvious that dope had edged out love in this race. Still I howled when we fucked that night, and Cynthia shot me dirty looks the next morning.

"Don't worry," I told her. "I never screamed like that with Timothy."

"You are such a tramp," she said.

"Could be worse," I answered. "I could be stupid."

Later Steve told me he thought I got off on being mean.

"No, I don't," I said, worried he might be right.

Mary and I left the others to babysit the kids, and we headed down to Tijuana. I drove down the hill from her apartment to the border—amazed at how easy it is to get in. I didn't have money, but Miss Mary had a little. While we waited for her connection to show, we sat around drinking in a bar called the Blue Note, where this guy she had the hots for played the drums. There were Christmas lights around the mirror but otherwise it was a lot like any neighborhood bar. I didn't like to drink, but Mary got me these things called zombies which tasted more like fruit punch. The sensation I felt was so different from dope that I started losing contact with myself. As the day wore on, neither of us wanted to go back to her apartment, to the crying children or the angry Cynthia or even to Timothy and Big Steve. I was looking at the Mexican men, thinking how fine they were with their black hair and brutal lips.

But finally it was getting dark, we'd been to the bakery for the sweet bread that the Mexicans call pan, and I tried Mexican ice cream, which, I must say, was on a par with Mexican heroin for absolute perfection. Mary had some dope in a rubber up in her vagina. I thought about how she left me in Tijuana that time. There was no way I was leaving her.

At the border we flirted with the guards. We showed them the things we'd bought—some embroidered shirts, a cloth purse. We admitted that we drank a bit too much but hey, we're tourists right? One of the guards leaned down and put his face close to Mary's.

"What are you doing later?" he asked. She looked sideways in this coy way and then said maybe she'd come back down after she'd gone to her hotel for a shower. And she smiled so sincerely, I almost believed she meant it. Perhaps for that split second she did mean it. I realized I had fallen for her ruse just like that stupid border guard. We were all chumps in Mary's world. She was a worthy teacher.

Then we were in my car, climbing the hill up to her apartment. When we walked in the door, there were six or seven junkies waiting to buy some dope. Mary went into the bathroom and came out, doled out a few shots.

"Come on, Trish," she said. She and I headed back to the bedroom. We were like lovers without the complications of sex.

We've both gotten off and are sitting on the floor, talking about the Mexican men.

"You're too friendly," she tells me. "They all think you want to sleep with them."

"That's asinine," I say, embarrassment buried under my numbness. Just then Big Steve starts banging on the door.

"Trish!" he yells. "Gimme the keys. This bitch has OD'ed."
I hear the words but the meaning doesn't register.
"It's their culture," she says. "Believe me, I know. I was married to one, and had kids with two others."
Big Steve continues banging on the locked door. I stare at it for a minute. Then Mary says, "Shit." She gets up.
"Hurry up!" Big Steve says. "I need the keys."
Mary opens the door.
"I don't know where my fucking keys are," I tell him.
"Trish, find your keys," Mary says. "I can't have this chick dying in my place."
The keys are up on the dresser. I take them out to the living room. Timothy is giving a heavy-set girl mouth to mouth. I remember the girl saying something about having just gotten out of the joint. Timothy pukes. Big Steve looks at me and he's all pissed off. The baby girl is screaming. The little boy is pretending like he's shooting us with a cap pistol. Justina sits in a corner and sucks her thumb.
I hand the keys to Big Steve and go back into the bedroom. Mary follows me.
Later that night Big Steve comes back and we sit outside on the hill overlooking the border.
"Did she die?" I ask him.
"I don't know," he says. "We just dropped her off at the emergency room. Didn't stick around. What kind of idiot shoots that much dope after going clean for six months. See all that jailhouse fat on her?"
"Yeah," I tell him, but I'm copping a nod, and I don't care about the fat girl. I don't care about anything.

The next day, Big Steve and I took Justina to the San Diego Zoo. Timothy and Cynthia stayed at Mary's and fought with each other. Mary had gone to see her parole officer.
It was one of those pretend-you-are-normal-people days. Justina played with my hair whenever we sat down. She gave names to all the monkeys. Eating cherry sno-cones, we watched the orangutans watch us from their plastic boulders.

Big Steve held my hand while we walked along the wide walk ways, Justina prancing ahead of us. Justina's eyes were wide and she was full of talk. I studied her buttermilk skin, her smile that would flash like sunlight caught in a mirror, and the way she danced with life about to burst from her body. She was a rare one, that kid.

"Did you have a good time, Justina?" Big Steve asked her in the car, heading back to Mary's.

"Yeah," she said. "I want to go again tomorrow and yesterday." She sat in the back seat, and I reached my hand back there to tickle her leg. She giggled madly. It was a good moment. I thought about the times my mom took me to the zoo. There was a picture of me with my hair in braids, wearing a sweater. I hardly ever smiled in pictures as a child, but maybe that's because children behave like themselves in front of a camera, and I wasn't much of a smiler as a kid.

When we got back, Timothy and Cynthia seemed to have come to some kind of understanding—about me, I guess. The house was clean, and they had made barbecued chicken and mashed potatoes. We all made an effort to be nice to each other. I made a couple of pies—a chocolate and a lemon. Everyone said the pies were great. But that night, Mary said she had to talk to me.

"We can't stay at Mary's," I told the others the next morning as we sat around the living room eating corn flakes. "She says there's too much heat with all these people coming and going."

Justina heard me, and she walked out of the room.

"Yeah, yeah, that's cool," Timothy said.

"Thank God," Cynthia said. "I'm gonna kill these rotten brats if we stay here another day."

I thought about Justina and I wondered if she'd be all right. Mary loved her kids, but they couldn't compete with the dope. I felt myself getting sad about it, so I zipped it up, pushed it away, forgot about it, thought about where the next shot was coming from. We still had some money left over from Jacksonville where we all had managed to borrow or steal a hundred or so bucks. But that would run out soon. Still, San Diego was a navy town. And we could always start beating sailors.

"We'll go to the Golden West," Timothy said. "The rooms there are cheap."

Mary said she'd see us down at the pier at Ocean Beach.

“I’m glad we’re outa there,” Big Steve said after we were settled into the Golden West Hotel in downtown San Diego. “Now maybe you won’t be running off to see your Mexican boyfriend anymore.”

“What the fuck are you talking about?” I asked.

“You know,” he said. “I can smell Mexican all over you whenever you come back from there.”

“All I did was dance with one of them one time,” I said.

“Sure,” he said. “Sure.”

In Ocean Beach the junkies ruled. I met one stringy-haired girl who had a set of tracks on her arm as thick as a rope. I finally understood why they were called tracks, because Southern Rails could have made a detour on her arm and never known the difference. A big purple ridge from elbow to wrist. In Florida we could buy fresh needles with relative ease, but in California it wasn’t legal so they had to use old hard-pointed needles and it was like pounding a chisel into your vein. They were all sculptors, neo-Rodins, using their bodies for marble. Our Florida arms were clean looking, maybe a little bruisy, but nothing like these thick California ridges.

In Ocean Beach we lived on ice cream and pizza, and the junkies strolled around with venom leaking from the side of their necks, saying this person was a snitch, or that person had V.D. I guess we thought we were members of the French court or something, skewering each other with lies and innuendo. Then again you never in your life met anyone more charming than a junkie who wants something from you.

One day Timothy tried to beat some sailors down at Ocean Beach. They kept ignoring his bullshit, and so he reached into the guy’s car and yanked a paper bag from the front seat. He threw it up in the air over to Big Steve and yelled, “Hey, bro’, it's full of pot!" Then he ran off with the sailors chasing him. Big Steve and I headed the other way. We looked inside the bag and found a bunch of dirty socks and underwear.

Big Steve and I laughed till we cried. Which was good, because we weren't laughing much in those days. We had little money and less love.

Like a Setting Sun

After the chaos of Mary's apartment with the screaming children and the junkies dropping by whenever, the room that Big Steve and I had at the Golden West was almost like a tomb in its quietness. Even though the seediness of the old hotel, once a grand haven for the wealthy, appealed to me, I felt haunted when we were in our room. Timothy and Cynthia had a room on another floor. We all figured it was better not to be in each other's faces for a while.

We sit on the twin beds and I look over at Big Steve. He seems unfazed by anything. Now that we're alone, we can't think of anything to say to each other. Big Steve starts clipping his toenails. I go to the window and stare down at the busy streets of San Diego below us. This room suddenly feels tight around me. I want to get out, but I don't know where I'd go. I wonder what my mom is doing back home. She gets so worried about me it gives her migraines. I'm always trying to escape that worry of hers, but now here it is, crawling around the back of my neck. Maybe it's because of Justina, but something tells me my life wasn't so bad back there. I think of coming home after school, smelling chili cooking, Mozart on the stereo. The silence in this room seems to pull the floor out from under me. We don't even have any books to read.

Big Steve pulls out a balloon of dope.

"What are you doing?" I ask him.

"What's it look like?" he says.

"Shit, can't you wait until later? We just got off this morning. Why not wait until that wears off?" I ask. I still feel a little nauseous from our wake up shot.

"Don't feel like it," he says.

I walk behind him and see the big pile of dope in the cooker. My stomach tightens on nothing.

"You know we don't have much money left, babe," I say, more insistent. "We're gonna feel really bad tomorrow if you shoot all the dope today."

"We'll worry about that tomorrow," he says. And then he pulls a full barrel of dope into his syringe and I watch him find his old reliable vein.

"Fucking asshole," I mutter and lie down on the bed.

Something drops on the floor, and I look back over at him. He's in the chair, sitting by the little desk where the cooker and the empty balloon lie. The syringe is on the floor.

"For God's sake, aren't you even going to clean out the works?" I ask in irritation.

But he doesn't answer me. I can see a fine thread of drool coming from his bottom lip. I get out of the bed and pick up the needle from the dirty linoleum floor.

"What the hell, Steve?" I say to him. Then I look at his eyes and they're doing this strange kaleidoscope thing and he babbles something at me.

"Shit!" I rush into the bathroom and get a glass of water. I run back in and splash the water on his face. His eyelids droop.

"Don't do this, baby," I say, shaking him. I need help. Where the hell is Timothy, I'm thinking. I don't have time to run to his room. Big Steve slumps down.

"Come on, baby," I say to him, coaxing him. I pull him from the chair and he stumbles with me into the bathroom. He's heavy, but I manage to push him into the tub where he lies like a sack of concrete. I turn the shower on but he's barely breathing. His eyes are swirling!

"Shit, shit, shit, shit, shit," I whisper. I get into the shower and lean over his big motionless body. His breaths come in irregular gasps. I start to push his chest and then I blow into his mouth.

"Come on, sweetheart, stay with me," I tell him. The cold water runs over my back and down through the soft swirling hairs of his chest. I redden his face with little slaps. And then I blow into his mouth again and again.

It seems like years before I feel his hands grab my wrists. He takes a deep breath and his eyes stop swirling. I pull away and turn off the shower.

"Why am I all fucking wet?" he asks.

"You did too much." I get off him and sit down on the toilet, trying to slow down my panicky heartbeats. Tears gather like old relatives in my eyes.

"I did not," he says and gets out of the shower. He strips off his drenched clothes. I stare up at him.

"I just saved your life, damn it," I say.

"I was all right," he says angrily. He walks out of the bathroom. "You fucked up my high."

I look down at the black and white tiled floor. There are old blood stains on the floor. The room is cold, and my skin is so pale, I can see right through myself.

Then I see that Big Steve has given me the answer to a question I didn't even know I was asking. I get up, go into the room, find my purse and go downstairs to use the pay phone. I don't even care that my clothes are soaked.

"I'm going home tomorrow," I told the others when we met that night in the diner of the Golden West. The only other patrons were a few garrulous old winos. "My mom is getting me a pre-paid ticket. Y'all can keep the car."

"Thanks, Trish. Did you know all the oil leaked out?" Timothy said.

"Why are you going?" Big Steve wanted to know. I couldn't tell if he was upset or not, if he wanted me to stay or not, but it didn't matter. Like a little, gray pigeon, my mind had a lock on home.

"My mom is sick," I told him. "I need to be there." The one true thing I can tell you is that most junkies love their moms. They bleed their mothers' bank accounts like starving leeches, but they still love them. So they didn't argue with me. Besides, I would be one less arm to feed.

Cynthia shrugged her shoulders. I knew she was happy to see me go. The next day, they took me to the airport. Big Steve gave me a long kiss good-bye. I wrapped my arms around his neck one last time. I had almost loved him, and I thought that he had almost loved me, too, but it was over. I was going home.

Crazy

As the jet descended, I looked down and saw the green felt landscape hurtling toward me. We were landing at the new "international" airport. When I was growing up, Jacksonville had a green airport with a big green control tower. The airport had a name—Imeson. This new airport did not have a name or a color. I had been absurdly attached to the green control tower. But then as a child I had imbued many buildings with the romance of feelings and imaginary associations. I remembered another tower. An old square tower that looked like a piece of a castle, a ruin. It sat by the street on the old DuPont estate, and every time we rode by it after we took my brother to school, I would ask my mother to stop so I could wander around those sand-colored walls and pretend I was its lost princess. If I had been Rapunzel I would never have let down my hair. I would have stayed up in the protection of my tower forever. That is what I most desired, a stone tower impervious to the world's brusque cuffs.

My mother waited for me in the gate area. Our eyes locked—mine guilty and yet still defiant, hers filled with determined despair, an incongruity only she could accomplish. We didn't hug. I wasn't sick yet, but I knew the bear was lurking a few steps behind me. And after the dope in California, I was pretty sure there was nothing in Jacksonville that would stand between me and it.

"I need to kick, Mom," I told her when we got into the warm car. "And I can't do it by myself."

She took a deep breath, reached over and stroked my arm lightly, and then turned the ignition.

"I've arranged for you to go to the hospital," she said, thumbs nervously tapping the steering wheel. I thought about that stone tower again.

She took me to the hospital where I was born and checked me in to the mental ward, which was the only place that would handle drug addiction. My mom knew how to do this, how to hang on to my life for me. My own grip was slipping.

A tall blond nurse took my bag, and led us into a semi-private room at the end of the hall. She gave me that look that said she knew I was a piece of shit, but she wouldn't show it with my mom around. I shrugged it off. As far as I was concerned, a nurse was simply a life support system for a needle.

I went to the window. Outside the blue-brown river had somewhere to go.

"I don't know why you don't give up on me," I said to my mom after the nurse left us alone. I must have been feeling remorseful. This little cure couldn't be cheap. Of course with me, remorse was bound to be a fleeting emotion.

"Because I see the you that you can't see anymore," she answered. I looked into her hazel eyes. Those eyes were keeping me alive. I thought about all the secrets I kept secret. I never even told her when my period started or asked her to buy me a bra.

Mom hugs me tightly before she goes.

I start unpacking my bag, and two women come in and sit on the other bed to stare at me. One of them is in her late 20s. She's my roommate, I gather, from the way she sprawls on the bed and takes a pack of cigarettes out of the table drawer next to her. The other looks to be about 17, has kind of stringy hair and can't seem to take her eyes off me.

Finally, I just stare back at the two of them.

"I'm Cheryl," the older woman says, fiddling nervously with a Winston.

"Trish," I say.

"Wud?" the younger woman asks, staring closely at my face.

"Trish," I repeat.

"Twish?" she asks.

I look over at Cheryl. Cheryl is smelling her cigarette.

"She's hard of hearing," Cheryl says. "But she ain't dumb. Her name's Deenie."

"Oh," and I examine the hard-of-hearing girl. She smiles at me, and I smile back.

"Come on, let's go to the dayroom and smoke a cigarette," Cheryl says. Her hand shakes a little. I've got nothing on my dance card, so I follow.

That night after the nurse gives me a shot of Demerol, the deaf-ish girl and I head into the visiting room to play a game of pool. I'm amazed at what good stuff Demerol actually is. Maybe I could stay here forever. The visiting room is long with windows looking out toward the other section of the hospital. We nutcases have our very own building. There's a pool table, some beanbag chairs and a couple of couches.

"Why are you here?" I ask Deenie.

"Coco," she answers. Now, that one throws me. I imagine her snorting up lines of Nestlé's Quik.

"Cocaine?" I ask.

"Yes, coco," she says. I decide not to pursue it any further. She doesn't seem "crazy," per se.

Deenie studies the tips of the pool cues, trying to find a couple that will actually work. And then my radar goes up. Even Demerol can't seem to dampen my dick-detector. I turn around and there's a youngish guy in a white outfit. He's got a neatly trimmed beard and dark hair. Looks smart, educated. Fine, I think, just fine.

He smiles. Well, he's got to. He's one of the zoo keepers, and we're the dangerous animals. But before long it's evident he actually likes us. He shoots a game of pool with me and Deenie. She wins. Then we're all sitting on the couch, and I'm telling him my life story, while Deenie tries to follow our lips.

What I find out about him is that he's a Gemini. And he goes to college during the day. He's studying psychology. I don't ask if he's got a girlfriend. He doesn't tell.

The next day we go to occupational therapy. I make an ashtray for my mom out of little tiles. I know she still smokes sometimes. Then I make one for Mary. For some reason, I miss Mary more than I miss Big Steve or Timothy.

In the afternoons, we play music on a stereo in the visiting room, disco shit, but Deenie can dance like she was born for nothing else. Really sexy—a little bent-knee, straight back shimmy.

Every morning and every night I get my shot of dem, and otherwise the highlight of the day comes when I get some time with the Gemini man. I start convincing myself that after I get out of the hospital, I'll really be cured. Never shoot dope again. Then I could snag a guy like this—a straight guy. What would we do, I wonder? Go to movies, dinner, talk about books and politics, I guess. It all seems possible when the Demerol saturates my blood.

My wing of the ward houses only women. Cheryl is here for attempting suicide. We're sitting around one evening, smoking cigarettes and talking about what a fat fuck the psychiatrist is when this middle-aged woman shuffles into the room. The rest of us all have on regular street clothes, but she's wearing fuzzy pink slippers and a quilted pink bathrobe. Her hair is dark, her face is puffy and blank.

"What the hell is wrong with her?" I ask Cheryl. Cheryl has blond hair and a constantly morose expression on her face, not to mention the white bandages around her wrists.

"Electric shock," she says, scratching her long nose.

I look at the woman. She doesn't say anything, just shuffles, keeping close to the walls, touching things as if she's trying to figure out where she is and what the objects around her are. We could be in another universe for all she knows.

"God, I hope that never happens to me," I say. "Do you think she'll ever be normal?"

"What's normal?" Cheryl responds and shoots a long, twirly trail of smoke from her lips. "What about you? Where did you say you got your drug addiction?"

"California, we smuggled the dope out of Mexico," I tell her with unabashed pride. "Me, I smuggled it. But we got robbed."

"What a life," she says. "You could write a book."

Suddenly Deenie comes up to me and hands me a little paper cup full of pills.

"Twish, I found your meds over there," she says.

Now, I have no idea what's in these pills, and there's no reason in the world that I should take them, but that doesn't stop me. I pop them in my mouth and take a swig of Pepsi just as the nurse walks in. The nurse stares at me with her chin cocked to the side. Then she rolls her eyes and stalks over to me.

"I ought to have your stomach pumped," she says, snatching the empty paper cup from my hand.

I just shrug. I don't remember anything from the next two days.

After a week, I got bored. I wanted some visitors besides my mom. So I called the only person I could think of who might come see me and got him put on Deenie's visitor list. Jasper Collins.

On Saturday Jasper loped into the visiting room. His sandy hair had grown. His nose was crooked, but otherwise he looked all right. He wore his preppy looking outfit which fooled his dad maybe. He wasn't strung out, that much was obvious, but he wished he was.

I introduced him to Deenie.

"Are you getting any good drugs?" he asked.

"Demerol," I said.

"Can you give me some?" he wanted to know.

"No," I answered. "They give me shots in the ass."

Neither of us mentioned the motel incident.

"Why don't y'all blow out of here for a while?" Jasper said. Deenie read his lips and nodded. It seemed like just the kind of plan Jasper would come up with. "Come on. It's boring in this place."

So we pretended like we were just walking him to the elevator, but when the doors opened, we jumped on with him. The nurses stood there with their mouths open as the elevator doors closed, and we were gone, laughing like maniacs. We ran into the parking and leapt like Batman and Robin into his white Camaro that was missing the back bumper.

Jasper squealed the tires as we left the parking lot. Sunlight sizzled in waves up from the road. Jasper's car smelled of beer and smoke and wet carpet. Deenie and I hooted. I hung my head out the window and waved to perfect strangers.

"Where do y'all want to go?" Jasper asked.

I thought about it for a moment or two. Where would we go? I was feeling pretty good from the dem and we didn't have any money so it wasn't like we needed to cop any dope. We drove along Riverside Avenue with its big brick houses and leafy oak trees. Then I knew where I wanted to go.

"Five points," I said. "That bar in Five Points."

"You want to go to a bar?" Jasper asked.

"Yes," I told him. So he turned the corner and drove up to Park Street. We passed my elementary school—big yellow prison, foreshadower of things to come. Jasper parked the car outside the lounge, and we got out.

"You got any money?" I asked Jasper.

"A little," he answered.

"So buy us a drink," I said. "Come on, tightwad. I'll pay you back."

We eased into the bar.

"A sloe gin fizz," I said to the bartender, a woman with dull eyes. Jasper got a Bud, and Deenie ordered a bloody Mary. I wasn't sure Deenie was old enough but the bartender didn't blink as she poured that cheap well brand vodka into the glass.

I know why I wanted to go to that particular bar. My father had taken me there once when I was about four or five. At least I think he did. He had moved out when I was three, but somehow in my foggy memory I came to this bar with my father. He was a jazz pianist, and this was one of those places where he and his little combo performed. I liked to imagine that he had loved me and done things with me even if they weren't ordinary go-to-the-zoo things. So maybe he had brought me to this bar when I was little, or maybe he hadn't. Regardless, I felt right at home swiveling around on the red vinyl bar stool.

Early that evening, Deenie and I went back to the mental ward. We walked in nonchalantly, and I headed back to my room. A few minutes later, I heard a strange garbled screaming, and I went into the hall and saw Deenie fighting with three of the nurses. Then one of the male attendants came and held her while the nurses squeezed a straitjacket on her. I felt as if I was watching a movie in a foreign language. I didn't understand why she was screaming like that or why they had to put that thing on her, but I knew by the way the nurses blasted their eyeballs at me, they blamed me.

Somebody dragged Deenie away, and then they came for me. I did not scream. I did not want to wear the jacket. So I docilely let them lead into a padded cell with no bed, no nothing.

"No Demerol for you tonight," the nurse said. "We don't know what you did out there. There could be a reaction."

"This seems rather draconian to me," I told her. "I could be miserable for free."

She slammed the door shut. I spent the night holding onto my knees and trying not to shit on myself. Snot poured from my nose. And my spine wanted to crawl out of my body. I thought about Deenie, how much fun she was, and I wondered what I did to her out there. Is she really crazy, I wondered, or just wild-tempered?

The next day I got out of the padded room. The nurse gave me an evil look before she shot me in the ass with a big needle of sweet Demerol. Deenie and I played a game of pool. I didn't ask her about the day before. She just smiled at me; she had a sweet smile, full of goodness. I figured it was all right for her to go a little crazy once in a while. We decided maybe we'd hang out together when we got out, but we never did.

Before I checked out, the fine Gemini dude came into my room to see me. I was wearing my jeans and a too-big shirt and hadn't brushed my hair all day.

"For some reason, I want to kiss you before you leave," he said. I didn't get kissed by nice guys, so I was happy to oblige.

I got out of the hospital on a Friday—three weeks after I'd first gone in. My mom and I rode to her apartment in silence, as if we were both carrying these heavy stones and didn't have the energy to speak. That's how I felt anyway. Lonely. And sad beyond reason. The sunlight flickering on the river as we rode across the bridge couldn't touch me, my heart was a vault.

When we got home, I didn't know what to do with myself. My mother sat at her piano and began to practice, but after a few minutes she stopped, closed the cover over the keys and went upstairs. I opened up the newspaper and started looking for a yoke.

A few days later I got hired to work in a drive-through liquor store next to a bar featuring topless dancers. I also got a letter from the California State Penitentiary in Chino, California. Big Steve was back in prison. He loved and missed me, he said in the letter. Chino was full of Mr. Lonely Hearts.

I wore a tight green skirt that hit just above my knees, a brown and green jungle print shirt and Aigner pumps. My hair had grown past my shoulders. I'd put another couple of streaks in it. I had the divorce papers tucked in my purse. It was a shitty thing to do, but I figured it was more shitty to do by mail. Besides, I wanted to see Charlie.

The drive took three hours, but the sunshine fell like an amber broth on the landscape, and oak trees nodded in the breeze. The loneliness that had surrounded me ever since I got back from the hospital slowly dissipated. I'd written Charlie every week when he first went down, then after I met Big Steve it was more like every month. Then not at all during the cross-country travels. Now the end of summer was approaching, he'd been locked up way longer than we'd lived together as a married couple.

I got to the prison—smack in the middle of orange groves. I couldn't see much but some low buildings that could have been almost anything. At the control room, those guys in their brown uniforms looked at me as if I was made of pure air. I had to go in a small room with a woman who patted me down. I walked through two gates, observed the curls of wire rolling over the fences. An enormous bank of blue grey clouds built up like pillars toward the east. What must it be like to live here, I wondered?

I sat at a square table in a big room with a linoleum floor, and after what seemed like forever, Charlie sauntered in, dark hair combed slick, blue uniform pressed. The uniform matched his eyes. He somehow made prison clothes look fashionable. He sat down with a sneer that passed for a smile.

"Hey, baby," he said in that soft drawling voice. "You look nice. Real nice." He said this with a sort of pulsing ache that ever so momentarily made me want to rip up those papers in my purse.

"It's been a long time," he said.

He lit a cigarette. I took a drag.

"It's all right," he said. "I'm glad you came. Hey, come on. Let's get our picture taken."

So we got a Polaroid taken of us. Then I had to pay the guy three dollars for the picture. I also bought us each a drink from the machine. I was glad I had come, glad to see Charlie, the hard look of his face, the soft look in his eyes.

His hands kept reaching for me, touching my leg, my arm.

I couldn't help wishing that things had been more like this when he'd been a free man. We talked some. He told me that an old girlfriend had written him and sent him a naked picture of herself. I felt no jealousy, just a mild amusement and gratitude for the subtle lesson: If you send a man in prison a naked picture of yourself, you can be sure he'll tell others, even his wife.

"Charlie," I told him. "I brought the divorce papers with me."

He glanced away. The sunlight gleamed on his hair. A moment later, he turned back to me, blue eyes dark as thunderclouds.

"I knew you would," he said.

"Charlie, it's worse to stay married. You know that," I said, leaning forward. He knew what I meant. I didn't have to say it. He saved face this way. He knew about Big Steve, and he knew there'd be others. He took my hand and stared down where there once had been a wedding band.

"All right, I'll sign them," he said. "But you gotta do me a favor."

I nodded. He looked at me intently, and it was the same old Charlie I'd always known, calling me "pretty lady" and wanting something. Then he averted his eyes the way a kid does when he's getting ready to lay on the big con.

"I want you to send me some reefer," he said.

"Brilliant," I said. "You're a real fucking Einstein. Ten years is not nearly enough fun. You need another sentence?"

"Listen to me," he said, leaning close, his hand gripping mine. "All you got to do is go to the newspaper office downtown and buy a newspaper, flatten out the baggie, stick it inside the paper and wrap it back up. Then have the newspaper folks mail it out from their mailroom. You can't possibly get caught. Baby, do this for me."

I found myself staring right into his sky-blue eyes. Sweet Jesus, he was good. I knew I would do it. I hadn't done much for him, but this I would do. Even if it sent me to the woman's prison right across the street.

Before I left, he kissed me and my fingers went up to his face, felt the skin against the hard bones, touched his neck and then brushed his arm.

Driving away from the prison was like driving through a long starless night. I felt clean now that it was over, but sad, too, wishing that we hadn't ever been married in the first place because now I could see how pointless it had been. The next week I sent him the pot.

Silver Spoon

I sat behind the red Formica counter in the liquor store, reading *Valley of the Dolls*, which was a lousy book but hard to put down. I'd just gotten to the part where some gorgeous woman offs herself when this chick walked in. The store was small, dingy red carpet on the floor, a cooler of cheap beer in the corner and shelves of bottles on the wall behind me. She was about my age, and she ordered a quart of Jack Black. I put the bottle in a bag and rang up the sale on the old cash register. Then she looked at me quizzically.

"You're Charlie's wife, aren't you?" she asked.

"I was," I said, a little surprised, and studied her: platinum blonde hair, pale skin, a long nose with a little hook on the end, wicked witch grin.

"I'd heard you were back in town, working here. I'm Angie," she said.

That name had floated out of Charlie's mouth a few times with an ironic bite that I could never quite decipher. That name had shrouded this woman and made her as mysterious as a spy. Now she stood in front of me with laughing eyes.

"Hey, how ya doing?" I asked, my fingers rubbing the side of the cash register.

"I'm O.K. Got a date out in the car. Some old fart."

I looked over her shoulder through the glass door and saw an gray man in an Olds 98. I looked back at her. Her lips canted in a funny way. I wanted her to stick around, talk some. This job was boring as hell.

"Charlie told me you wrote to him," I said.

Her lips twitched.

I said, "Hell, I don't care. He's in prison. I'm glad you wrote him. Must be lonely in there."

I could see the question on her face. She was wondering if he had told me about the naked picture. I thought it was strange that she'd send him a naked picture of herself. I wouldn't do it even when I was married to him. But I didn't hold it against her. I hadn't exactly been Sweet Polly Purebread, tying yellow ribbons around the old oak tree.

Angie shot me a wide, red-lipped smile, uncovering an armament of pointy white teeth.

"Say, can you cop some dope?" she asked.

"Yeah, I guess," I answered when, of course, that was exactly what I had planned to do that night. I didn't have a habit anymore, but the first time I got my period after getting out of the hospital had seemed a good time to get some medicinal treatment. I'd gone to the street corner doctor, and been visiting a couple of times a week ever since.

"Wait right here," she said, leaning over the counter, squinting her eyes at me.

"I'm not going anywhere," I said. "At least not until eight o'clock."

Angie dashed out the door. She was all energy, hair flying, crimson lips and electric green eyes. In a few minutes, she came back with some bucks in her hand.

"If you get me four bags, I'll give you one," she said, holding out the money like a bouquet of paper flowers.

"Two," I said. The blue neon sign in the window flashed sporadically.

"Deal."

I reached out my hand for the money, and we both held onto it for a second before she released it.

"I'll meet you back here at nine," I said. "Out front."

The liquor store was on a desolate piece of highway heading out of town. It was a good place to work because I never ran into people that I used to know. It wasn't the sort of place any of my mother's friends would stop by to pick up a bottle of good wine. Next door was a lounge that featured topless dancers 2 p.m. to 2 a.m. Sometimes the bartender would come over to refill her stock of well brands and we'd chat a little bit. Once she brought over a sloe gin fizz for me.

The customers who came to the liquor store were mostly guys by themselves pulling through the drive-in lane in a pickup truck or an old beater of a car for a six-pack or a single Tall Boy. They'd give me a tip of a quarter or so. In between customers I'd read. There was a black guy I hung out with sometimes, an old friend of Charlie's who would cop heroin for me. We would sit around the little shotgun house where his mother lived, and if I was too fucked up to drive home, I could stay the night, and in the mornings she'd make cornbread in an iron skillet and smear it with butter. I discovered I liked most black people better than most white people, but Jacksonville whites and blacks didn't care for you to cross that boundary too many times, and so I kept a low profile.

I got back to the liquor store about nine-fifteen, and I thought Angie would piss on herself in excitement. She had gotten rid of the old fart and was by herself, tapping red nails on the roof of a sleek black car, drumming an old, old song.

"I swear I thought I'd never see you again," she said, laughing the way you do when the tension has made your stomach feel like it's full of jelly beans. "I just knew that you really hated me for that damn letter. I knew you had beat me."

I looked at her blankly. It had never occurred to me to rip her off, and I wondered why not. We were standing in the parking area right in front of the liquor store, not far from the flashing sign by the side of the road that said “Girls, Girls, Girls! Toples Dancers!” Personally I loved the misspelling.

The October darkness had settled almost like an afterthought. I stood there holding the little pieces of tin foil cupped in my hand. The old-time dopers always said the dope was better if you mixed it all together. That's because they figured they could always beat you out of a little smidgen, but still we believed it anyway. Four bags of dope cooked together yielded a better high for two people than two bags of dope cooked separately.

"Where can we get off?" she asked.

"My place," I said, meaning my mom's apartment. She got in her car followed me to my mom's. Mom was downstairs watching television. She had that startled looked that she always got whenever I came home. Startled and a little fearful and ready for anything. The unspoken understanding was that whatever I did she would rather me do it there in the zone of maternal protection.

Angie stood in the living room, checking it out. In an earlier generation we would probably have been described as living in genteel poverty. We had a few valuable musical instruments—a French horn and a cello—hundreds of books, a few antiques and some nice pictures, including a Rembrandt sketch, but our apartment was middle of the road and private school had been paid for through scholarships.

Mom was nice to Angie, smiled at her and said in that perfectly enunciated way of hers, "How do you do?"

Angie shook my mom's hand, oohed and ahhed over the Duncan Phyfe dining table and the Steinway, and then finally followed me up the blue carpeted stairway. I showed her into my room. I had a double bed, a bookcase, a desk, a TV, and a coffee table. I slipped into the bathroom and got the water. My needles were in my coat pocket in my closet. Everything was ready. I locked the door, we sat down and I lit a candle. Angie looked over at my books.

"Your mom seems so refined. Where's she from?" she said, browsing the titles.

"Connecticut," I answered. "She went to Yale."

"No shit," Angie said.

"My brother's into music, too. He conducts a small-town symphony."

"What about you?" Angie asked.

I held up the needle.

"I'm a fucking maestro," I said.

She laughed. I scraped the bags of dope into an old bottle cap and started cooking.

"Does your mom know what we're doing?" Angie asked.

I shrugged.

"She's spent most of her life living with alcoholics," I answered. "One parent. Two husbands. Living with a dope fiend is probably easier. At least I'm not violent when I'm high."

"I guess you're right," Angie said.

When you get off with someone, it means something. You are entering a pact, sealing your friendship or your love like children who prick their fingers and become blood brothers or blood sisters. You perform the secret rituals together, mixing water and drug, administering the fire. You raise the needle like a chalice. You are witches, sorcerers, priests.

Later, when you betray each other, it is a violent and personal act.

Angie drove a black Mustang, and she would whoop and holler in glee--especially if we were on our way somewhere to get off. Her favorite song was "Shooting Star" by Bad Company. She liked the "shooting" part of it. She had the lousiest veins which is why our friendship became so solid, I suppose, because I was a top-flight nurse with a needle. The whole process was fascinating to me. You could slide a needle into that blue tube on someone's arm, red blood would leap into the needle signifying a hit and with just a small amount of liquid injected into your blood stream, everything would become totally different. A soft warm fog would descend around you or else you'd be on a rocket ship through the cosmos, depending on the drug. Heroin, of course, was the natural Zeus reigning at the top of this powdery Mount Olympus. It would lead you to wander in the netherworld for hours, consorting with spirits and demons. When you came back up, the utter rawness of life felt like a freezing cold shower.

One day we needed a place to get off. We drove by the church where Jasper's dad was a priest, and I thought it would be cool to get off inside. Luckily, Jasper was home, and for the price of a bag of dope, he took us into the church through the back door. We went up a flight of steps and into a some kind of dressing room for the choir. Jasper disappeared and then returned with a cup of water.

"Holy water," he said.

We cooked the dope in an old bottle cap that I took everywhere with me. I searched for a vein on Angie's fleshy white arm, and as I jabbed the needle in, the vein ran away from me.

"Calypso," she sang. Then I got the vein, and I shot the dope in fast because I was scared of losing it.

"Jack it, daddy," she said. "Jack it back."

She wanted me to give her a boot, to pull the blood back and then reinject it—dope fiends think this will get you higher. Charlie would boot for hours, needle hanging from a vein on the back of his arm. But nobody talked in such crazy lingo. I mean, "daddy"?

"Did you bring her back with you from the hospital, Trish?" Jasper asked me when she excused herself to go to the bathroom.

I just scratched my nose and shrugged it off. Angie was smart, way smart; no one except me knew it. I thought I could see Mephistopheles shining in her eyes when I looked closely.

"My father is crazy," Angie told me.

"So?" I asked.

"Don't you see?" she said. "It's in me, too. I know I'm going to be just like him."

I thought about it, but didn't answer her. I didn't know what it was like to have a crazy father. I didn't know what it was like to have any father at all. My so-called father was an absence, a black hole, a memory of my mother falling like a felled pine. He was locked doors, phone calls late at night, court appointments—all things that were vague and shadowy. Things from my childhood that my mother might allude to but never outright tell me.

"You like poetry, Trish?" she asked, looking over at my books.

"Yeah, I do," I answered. "I like T.S. Eliot."

"Oh, me, too. I like that one about the patient etherized against the sky," she said.

"The one with those chicks always talking of Michelangelo," I said.

"What kind of women do you suppose those were?" Angie asked. "Whores?"

I scratched my nose.

"Nah, society bitches," I said.

"Same thing," Angie said. We nodded off for awhile, and then I roused myself.

"Did you love Charlie?" I asked her.

"Yeah, I did. I lost my virginity to him. He plucked my maidenhood," she said dreamily. Sometimes I thought she must have been reading those supermarket romances on the sly.

Angie and I never went shopping together or to the movies or the beach. The only thing we did was shoot heroin, sometimes mixed with cocaine, and sit around my mom's apartment. Sometimes we'd talk about poetry. She went on a real Sylvia Plath jag, and she'd read the poems out loud, spitting out the words like a pissed-off cat. Other times we'd talk about men.

One night we went out and sat on the dock that belonged to the apartment complex. I loved going there, especially when I was high. The river slid by, gnawing on the wooden posts. That's when Angie first mentioned the Wiggins boys, Hank and Roy. Charlie had said to stay away from them so naturally I was curious.

"They're fine, Trish," Angie said, nodding her head and scratching her nose, "You can have Roy, and I'll take Hank." I didn't have any kind of love life going, so this mythical Roy gave me something to think about.

Angie got a job working for a doctor and she'd come over afterwards, wearing her white uniform. Then she'd borrow my clothes—the most expensive ones I had. We went to bars once in a while though I hated to drink. Once a couple of old guys took us to a Holiday Inn to go dancing, and we danced with each other instead of them. It was fun. The looks that people gave us. Fat-faced, squinty-eyed Jacksonville glares that said "Lookit those lesbos." We kept asking our "dates" for money for drinks, going up to the bar and getting coca-colas and pocketing the change from a ten or twenty. As soon as we could, we ditched the old guys and went downtown and bought some heroin.

I hadn't called her in a few days. Jasper Collins had stolen some Dilaudids from his terminally ill great aunt, and I was helping sell them--for a fee, of course. But one day Jasper was out of D's. I had a few bucks and decided to call Angie and ask her to come over. I needed a ride to go cop.

"No, Trish," she said. "You just use people. You use everyone."

Of course, I used people. I was a junkie. What other behavior would anyone expect from me? And didn't she use me, too?

"I'm sorry. I don't mean to use you," I said. Was that what I was supposed to say? Where was the script for this?

"Aw, you'll say anything right now because you want to cop."

She hung up on me, but a half hour later, she knocked on my door.

"Let's go, Daddy-o," she said.

Wasting the Time Away

Shannon's parents owned a big house on a bluff overlooking the river. They built an addition onto the house just for the teenagers, and we always called it the "new room." I practically lived there, spending the weekends and all the holidays with Shannon. Her parents weren't getting along.

Mom had her own problems with Richie, whose drinking problem had gotten worse and worse. He got cirrhosis of the liver and had to go someplace to dry out for a few weeks, but the day after he came back I found him tipping up a bottle of vodka in the kitchen. My mother seemed to age about ten years.

So we all hung out in the new room while our parents' lives fell apart. Jasper was always there, slouched on the couch, a shank of sandy hair falling into his eyes. He would most likely have a cigarette wedged between his lips. His eyes would twinkle with some mischievousness. And Shannon would be eating Fritos and dip and reading R. Crumb comic books.

A whole gang of us went to a Jethro Tull concert that year. We thronged on the floor of the stadium, swaying, dancing, throwing Frisbees. The smell of reefer hung like a barrier between us and the orange-vested police. For weeks afterward, we pretended to be flute players, standing like storks with one leg bent and a foot tap, tap, tapping the straight knee. Aqualung and Cross-eyed Mary were our heroes.

That year I felt that I was on the verge of opening up the world. I knew I wasn't there yet, but it wasn't far off, a year or maybe two, and then I'd know the secret of life. But not yet. I had a good feeling about life, about my life. I never once thought about sticking a needle into my arm. The drugs we did, marijuana and the occasional tab of mescaline, just colored the world the way we thought it ought to be, a beautiful

Crayola purple. Life was festive and funny, like birthdays every day.

Jasper, Shannon and I are skipping school. We sneak off from the sprawling campus of our school and catch a bus downtown. Then we walk across the Main Street Bridge, the old one that actually has a sidewalk. When we get to the top, we climb down the metal beams, which are painted sky blue, to a platform where we can dangle our legs high over the water. If we were to fall, it would surely kill us, but we are fourteen years old and nothing can touch us. The river flows carelessly by.

This is when we decide that Jasper will be a warlock and Shannon and I will be witches. Shannon has already been practicing with the Tarot cards. She wears thick black eyeliner and dark lipstick. Later on, I tattoo a pentagram in blue ball-point on Jasper's back. Jasper buys *The Satanic Bible* by Anton Lavey. But with Jasper, it's all a game. With Shannon, I can tell already that she's searching for something. So while we all play at witchcraft, casting spells on the teachers or the other kids we hate, Shannon is the only believes it. Jasper and I just enjoy getting stoned and listening to music.

One Two Three

I quit working at the liquor store and started hanging out more with Jasper, who had forged some refills of his great-aunt's scrip.

Sometime around Thanksgiving, he said he had to sell some Dilaudids to somebody. So we rode over to this steak house by the Matthews bridge. I didn't like the Matthews Bridge much. It was too round and didn't feel like my bridge. Not like the Fuller Warren Bridge or the long, winding Hart Bridge, which falls over the river like a ribbon someone let fall to the floor.

We pulled into the lot next to an old Cutlass. I was stone-eyed and foggy, so when Jasper introduced me to this guy all I heard was the name Wiggins. But that name got my attention. I remembered Angie talking about the Wiggins' boys. I could tell this guy in the other car had heard of me, too. Every junkie in town knew every other junkie--either personally or by reputation. Since I'd been to California, my stock had doubled.

I looked over at him, sitting behind the wheel of his old Cutlass. He was tall, red-cheeked and cocky looking. I wondered if this is the one Angie had a crush on or the one I was supposed to like.

He looked over at me, too.

"So you're Trish," he said. Then he said to Jasper, "You ought to get a haircut. You look like a fuckin' hippie."

"I am a hippie," Jasper said, pushing back his sandy curls.

"Not me. I'm a dope-shooting redneck," he said.

And then I laughed. The Wiggins fellow winked at me.

"Be seein' you around, huh?" Then he reached out and handed me a piece of paper with his phone number.

"Yeah, yeah," I said. We drove off and I asked Jasper was that Hank or Roy?

“How the fuck do I know?” Jasper said. “I can’t tell those hicks from each other. You know the oldest one is doing 30 in Raiford.”

I wondered if Jasper was jealous. Not of me liking the Wiggins boy, but because I had more of a reputation than he did. Jasper and I never had sex. It would have felt incestuous. But Jasper liked to think of himself as a bad dude, and he just wasn’t. He was the preacher’s boy, and he always would be.

A few nights later I had my hands on some Dilaudids that I’d gotten from a dentist. I was home, and I didn't want to get high by myself. Angie was unavailable, and I was sick to death of Jasper. So I called up the Wiggins boys, took a wild guess and asked for Roy.

"This is me," he said. His voice had a deep country twang.

“This is Trish,” I said. “Remember me? From the other night?”

“Sure I do,” he said.

"I got some D's," I said. "Want to go out?"

"I reckon. Where do you live?" he asked. I told him, and even though he lived clear across town, it wasn’t but a few minutes before I heard an old car rumble into the parking lot outside. A free Dilaudid is a powerful incentive.

I opened the door, and there was a guy I had never seen before in my life.

“Who the hell are you?” I asked.

“I’m Roy Wiggins,” he said. “You invited me over.”

"I thought you were the other one," I said. "The one I met the other night."

"No," he said. "That was Hank."

“You knew that’s who I thought I was talking to, didn’t you?” I asked.

He smiled. Roy was tall and lanky with dark reddish-brown hair, a triangle face, and the softest, most exquisite lips I had ever seen on a man. Dressed in high-water corduroys and a dark blue button-down shirt that was too small, he seemed as vulnerable as a kitten.

We got into his car, an old Impala, and I asked him where he was taking me.

"You want to go get a room?" he asked as he pulled out of the parking lot.

"Damn," I said. "Can't you at least take me out for a drink first?"

"All right," he said, "Where do you want to go?"

"Let's go by the Keg," I said. So we went to a bar back on the other side of town where a lot of people I knew went. Roy didn't fit in with this crowd, and I didn't either anymore. I knew them from high school, and they were mostly the kids of the rich or the almost-rich. They were drinking beer and playing foosball. Some people said hi to me. Others asked about Charlie. And others just looked at me like I was the cheese between their toes. After about fifteen minutes, we left and got a room at the Red Carpet Inn.

I loved motel rooms. Even cheap ones. The sheets are clean. Everything is anonymous. The television works. The door locks. You are alone and no one else knows where you are. I pulled a package of new works—8 100-unit insulin syringes, ¾-inch gauge—out of my purse and tossed them onto the bed nonchalantly. I placed the Dilaudids on the dresser.

"Fix those up," I said, and I went into the bathroom and drew myself a hot bath. I got into the bath tub and soaped myself with the tiny bar of soap. When I raised my leg out of the water, steam fell off my skin in streamers and I was reminded of something out of a Greek myth—a nymph running through Hades. I read all the Greek myths when I was a kid. The story of Persephone was my favorite. The way her mother trampled all over the earth to get her away from Hades. I could see my mom doing something like that if she only could. But since she couldn't, I supposed she'd follow me through it.

Roy knocked on the door. I had pulled the shower curtain to cover most of the bathtub.

"You want your shot now?" he asked, standing in the doorway. I nodded and held out my arm. He sat down on the toilet. I had my hair up in a ponytail on top of my head. Roy glanced past the curtain at me, lying naked in the tub, then he looked into my eyes.

"Did you do yours?" I asked. He scratched his nose and said, yes. I looked at his bare arms. He had long ropy veins. I squeezed my wrist and a good vein on the back of my hand popped up. Roy pricked the tough skin of my hand and got the needle into the vein. The vein rose a little bit, but he wasn't missing. The cool clean Dilaudid spread through me, and even there in the bathtub I could feel my vagina heating up as if a bright orange coil glowed inside me. My nose and my lips itched, and I wanted to be kissed.

I took the needle from him and cleaned it in the bathwater. He left the bathroom. I heard the television come on. I got out, wrapped a towel around my body, and went in to the room. I lay down beside him. Our legs touched. He had long country feet and strong, big-elbowed arms. He took my hand and we watched the TV until we fell asleep.

When I woke up, I saw him lying next to me asleep. He seemed so fragile. I touched his lips, and he woke up. When he looked at me, his eyes said something to me that had never been said before—not by Charlie, not even by Big Steve. It was as if he was just discovering me there lying in the bed next to him. Like I was another country. Like he was Magellan.

"You are such a doll," he said. And the words lolled out of his mouth like honey. His hands reached for me, roved over my breasts, spread open my legs. His deep kiss reminded me of body surfing in the Atlantic before a storm. We fucked for a long time, quietly in the thicket of sheets and blankets, until we finally kicked them off the bed and lay there wasted and satisfied like a pair of lions who have just eaten a gazelle.

Later we went to the Waffle House for breakfast.

"Tell me about your life," I said, leaving half a waffle on the plate. He had lit a cigarette. "You ever been anywhere?"

He had these sweet dark eyes that drifted across the table and then would look right back into mine.

"Saigon," he answered.

"You gotta be kidding," I said. "You were in the army or what?"

"Army. I was an E-5," he said.

"You killed people and all?" I was thinking of everything I'd been taught to think about Vietnam—it was wrong, the wrongest of all wrong things.

"Yeah, I killed people when I had to," Roy said in a voice as gentle as falling light. "I was the point man in my platoon. My mama prayed for me every morning. Guess that's why I'm still alive."

"Is that where you got your first habit?" I asked.

He shook his head, his lips doing this exaggerated frown thing that southerners do.

"No," he answered. "I didn't shoot no dope till I got home."

"You didn't?" I asked, thinking about all the stories, the songs, the legends of Vietnam vets and how heroin was the only way they could survive the horror.

"Naw," he said. "I liked Vietnam. Well, I liked Saigon. I liked the whores. They were sweet. Shit, I had never even had sex before. I'm usually too scared to ask anybody for some. A chick has to throw it on me before I'll take it."

"You didn't seem too scared this morning," I said.

He shrugged, smiled at me and let a long tube of smoke shoot through his lips. Then he said, "I was."

When he took me home, he kissed me and his lips were sticky with syrup and sweet tasting.

"Bye, doll," he said.

"I'll call you sometime," I said, getting out of the car.

"You better," he said.

I went inside my mother's cool blue-carpeted apartment and felt those eyes of his and his hand prints lingering on me. I went into the dining area and saw the remains of my mother's breakfast—a piece of toast, some orange marmalade on the edge of a black rimmed plate. She had also left out a bowl of cut up oranges, apples and bananas for me. This was her way of trying to keep me alive. I sat down and ate.

Roy lived with his momma and daddy and Hank and two younger brothers in a small house that was built right up on a ditch that ran alongside a truck route. They had a chain link fence around the property and a sign that said beware of the dog. Inside the fence three or four moth-eaten blue merle collies wagged happily at any visitor, and a slew of cats slept on and under the immovable Chevy Nova in the driveway. The Chevrolet belonged to the brother in prison and had not been driven since he was taken away by the police three years earlier.

That's what Roy explained to me the first time I came over.

"Well, I see Roy got to you first," Hank said when Roy showed me into the house. Hank was sitting at a long dining table. A dirty-faced child of indistinguishable gender crawled up onto his lap.

"This is my sister's baby," Hank explained. "I ain't got any young uns."

A woman came walking out of the kitchen, gingerly as if her feet hurt. She was gray-haired and plump with red cheeks and the brightest eyes I had ever seen. "Come in. Have a seat," she said. "You want some ice tea?"

That was Roy and Hank's momma. I later met his daddy, too, only the circumstances proved to be less than fortuitous.

There was a trailer back behind the house where one of Roy's sisters had lived with her husband for a while. We'd just scored a half load of dope and we needed a place to do our business. Roy and Hank decided we'd get off in the trailer. It was evening. The dusky sky sported a red stripe scratched across the horizon.

"Come back to the parlor," Hank said, walking with a jaunty legs-too-long walk. Now, I knew it must have looked strange the three of us traipsing past the house and going into that trailer that didn't even have any electricity anymore, but dope makes you bold as hell. You actually believe that everyone accepts whatever fantastic story spins out of your mouth.

We opened the squeaky metal door and stepped into the coop. The stale air barely made room for us.

"Well, this is a lovely place, y'all," I said.

Roy's hand found my back and he said, "We'll rent it to you. Cheap."

"The cockroaches cost extra though," Hank said, squashing a palmetto bug the size of sparrow.

I don't know. Maybe it was all that country-fried testosterone. I just enjoyed being with those boys. We turned on the faucet. Eureka! Water spurted out. We knew our routine, and in moments we had dope bubbling in the top of a bottle cap, we tossed in a piece of cigarette filter and each drew up about thirty units. Oh man, this was going to be sweet. Roy held my arm for me while I found a vein and then I slid into home base as he released the pressure on my arm. The dope takes maybe two seconds to hit and then you let out a little grunt, a hum of pleasure. The curtains open and the show you came to see begins.

After we'd had our shots, we were not nearly so efficient. We scratched faces, our voices lost clarity, and we fumbled in the dark to clean out the works. Hank drew up a syringe full of water and squirted it out the window.

"God almighty!"

We froze and looked at each other.

"Daddy?" Roy called out.

"What the hell are you doing in there? And who squirted water in my face?" Bloody water, I might add.

"It's just us, Daddy," Hank said.

"I know it's just you, and I know what you're up to. Y'all better get on out of there. I oughtta take a belt to all three of you," he said.

I couldn't see him. I hadn't ever seen him, but I could suddenly imagine some wild old man chasing around these grown boys and me with his leather belt, all of us screaming and trying to get away from him.

"Shit," whispered Roy.

"And stop cussing," the voice added.

We came out sheepishly. Roy's daddy was a small man, but powerfully built. I realized that if he did take off his belt, we might be in trouble. I was glad he caught us after the fact and not before. And I knew Hank and Roy felt the same way. It was all I could do not to scratch my nose.

"We were just showing her the trailer," Hank said.

"In the dark? You all must think that when God was handing out brains I thought he said trains. Is that what you think?"

"No, sir," Roy said.

Roy's daddy shook his head and walked inside the house.

"I think maybe we should go buy a pack of smokes," Hank said. So we got in my car, went down to the old gas station on the corner and sat in the car smoking cigarettes, drinking Pepsi and nodding off until we figured it was safe for them to go home. Then I had to drive all the way back to the other side of town, which wasn't easy on a good nod.

Cool, Cool Hand

A few days later, I called up Angie to see if she wanted to go out with me and Roy and Hank, but she just laughed.

"What's so funny?" I asked.

"Girl, you can forget those Wiggins boys," she said. "Come out with me tonight."

Her voice sounded creamy, like she had stumbled into some serious sin.

"Okay," I said. "Then come get me."

She did.

Angie had hooked a sugar daddy, a black man in his 50s, who was connected like a telephone pole. He had the best dope ever to come to Jacksonville. He had dope you could actually get a serious habit on. Thick brown Mexican mud, so dark and muddy it would clog the needle so you had to use the old kind of syringes, the kind with the detachable needle which allowed you to draw up the dope through the barrel.

Angie and I lost ourselves. We got monster habits. We slept all day and just went out a few hours at night to go to a motel room and shoot her sugar daddy's dope. Drool dripping from our lips, our eyes unable to see past about four or five feet in front of us, the languorous cocoon spinning around and around us. There was no reason to live; no reason to die. We stopped eating. We barely needed air.

On the long sleep-filled, dream-driven afternoons, while the heroin still percolated slowly in my system, my mother would come up to my room to make sure I wasn't dead. She would rub my back softly, her musical hands calling me back.

I see her standing by the piano, staring out through the sliding glass doors of the apartment at the thick green world outside, the drapy oak trees, the scalding blue sky, staring at nothing. She must have wondered what she had done wrong, why her daughter was slowly and methodically annihilating herself? Why hadn't the gymnastic lessons, the art classes, the books, the expensive school been enough? Perhaps she remembered holding me as a little girl, kissing the top of my head, smelling the perfume of childhood in my neck, and then saying, you are my precious one. She must have wondered why everyone she got close to was driving the wrong way on a one-way street.

My mother brought a psychiatrist over to the apartment. He was nice enough, but said there wasn't much he could do. He did know of a place, however. Then before I know it, I'm on a plane heading for a drug program in New York.

Till It's Gone

My brother, who had moved to New York a while back, rode with me in the back of the taxi cab through the city streets from the airport to the drug program on the outskirts of Harlem.

"Didn't you bring any gloves?" he asked.

"Who needs gloves in Florida?" I said.

"I remember some frosty mornings back then, going to band practice. You and Momma used to come watch," he said. I remembered those cold mornings, wrapped in my mother's coat next to her warmth as my brother and his fellow band members marched on the field with their horns and drums.

The taxi jerked through the traffic, and my brother reached over to squeeze my hand.

"Are you all right?" he asked. His voice sounded padded like a cell where they put crazy people.

"I'm fine," I said. I had a few more hours before the sickness hit.

The taxi cab pulled up in front of a brownstone building that looked like the apartment houses on either side except for the sign above the door with the name of the drug program. My brother brought my suitcases inside, and a guy whisked them into an office. Then the guy told my brother they'd take care of me and that I couldn't have any contact with anyone from the outside for the first three months, including him.

The first few days in the drug program were smooth--mellow and warm in an orange methadone blur even though every morning I had to walk twenty city blocks to get to the clinic. I strode down the dark New York streets, littered with trash, smelling of steam and cold. My silent escort went with me. I looked into the smoky windows of shops that we passed, thought about how different it was from Florida. Everyone I saw on the corners looked like a junkie to me. I wanted to ask them where I could cop, but Sir Snitch watched me all the time. Here I was in New York City and I had to suck down methadone every morning. I missed the rush of heroin, but methadone had its own fuzzy pleasure.

One morning as I was all bundled up in my flimsy Florida winter clothes, I opened the door of the house and a white wind shoved me back inside, slapping my face with whiplashes of cold. A storm, a monstrous, wounded polar bear, roared outside the door. With my body, I punctured a hole in the wall of wind and fell outside. Snow rushed around me in swirls. Still I trudged the twenty blocks in my soaking leather boots to get my fix and then lumbered back. I couldn't feel my toes. My hands and face were chapped and flinty as if I'd been scrubbed down with sandpaper. My escort didn't seem to mind. He was lanky and hard and dressed like a northerner.

The people who ran the drug program said I could stop going for the methadone if I wanted to, but I went all fifteen days. The last couple of days the dose was so low it didn't even last an hour.

A Puerto Rican woman ran the place. She'd entered the program when she was fourteen. It was her mother and her father. She had a wide, golden smile, but if you messed with her program, she was ruthless. The last thing you ever wanted from her was a "haircut,"—a verbal mauling that could be heard miles away as she told her hapless victim to "slither under the door like the piece of slime" that he or she was. The residents all called her Chief. She called me Scarlet, and a few of the guys moaned, "I'll never go without dope again" whenever they saw me.

Those first few weeks, I swept stairs—five flights of them—every day. In fact, we cleaned all the time. When we cleaned the main meeting room, we swept the corners, dusted the books that no one read, wiped the windows and mopped the floors. In the kitchen we scrubbed the chrome surfaces high and low, we cleaned the big grill with vinegar and water, we washed enormous pots and pans. The bathrooms sparkled.

In the evenings we all sat in the big living room in folding chairs and watched the news. I waited for glimpses of Jimmy Carter and the chance to hear his sweet southern drawl.

Once the methadone was gone, I couldn't sleep. I could hardly eat. My bones felt as if they were crumbling inside my body. My nose was a fountain of mucus. At night my legs jerked and ran while I lay there. I felt as if I were seeing the world through a screen door. Nothing was quite in focus.

A week or so after I got off the methadone, I was downstairs mopping the dining room floor when a voice came crashing down the stairwell like a set of china plates.

"All females to the fifth floor! All females!" the voice screamed. We scurried up the five flights of steps—all seven of us. The one doing the screaming was a longer-term level three resident. The longer you were there the more power you had over others.

"Who is the nasty, nasty female that left her stinking nasty underwear out here?" she screamed at us—all white teeth, stiletto eyes, rage jerking her limbs as if she was having a seizure. I grabbed the underwear and shoved it into my dirty clothes. Rivers of humiliation made a mess of my face. I should have laughed, but I just couldn't.

"Don't come crying to me," one of the other women said.

That night I lay in my bunk, homesick for the soft bed in my mother's apartment, for the easy smile on Roy's face after we'd just scored, and for the gentle hypocrisy that oiled every southern utterance. Every night I dreamed about heroin. It was a bird in my dreams, floating on air currents just out of my reach. I wondered about Charlie. Little images—that sneer of his, the shocking blueness of his eyes—visited me at the strangest moments. I thought about him in his prison bunk. I wondered if prison could possibly be worse than this.

I learned how to be careful. I never knew what landmine waited for my unwary foot. If I smiled at someone, they might tell me I was a hypocrite and a phony. If I didn't smile, then I had a bad attitude. If I talked to the guys, I would be accused of being "slimy." If I didn't talk to them, I had no one because the women didn't have much use for me—and vice versa.

Another month passed and I was still on cleaning duty, but the symptoms of my withdrawal had receded. Then one afternoon I mentioned that I could type. The next day they made me the secretary to the day counselor, a staff member who had gone through the program. Working in the program seemed to be what one did upon graduation. A dreadful prospect to me.

The day counselor was thin and gypsy-faced with a stubble on his pointed chin, dark, almost-black eyes and bony Dracula hands. He brooded a lot, but he had a shock of a smile that transformed his face. He'd been clean for two years, he told me. He still looked like a junkie to me. It was the gleam in his eye whenever he talked about all the dope he used to shoot. I was drawn to that gleam the way a cold person is drawn to a trash-can fire.

I sat at a small desk in his office and typed stuff. The door would close, his head would bend close to mine, his hands pressing against my shoulders.

"You know, " he told me one time. "I've known prettier girls than you and I've known smarter girls than you, but I've never known any that were prettier *and* smarter."

"Is that right?" I said.

"Who's your favorite writer?" he asked on another day.

"Faulkner," I answered. "Who else?"

"You should read Herman Hesse," he said.

So I tried to read Steppenwolf but reading was frowned upon in drug treatment. As was talking to the same person too much. During your free time you were supposed to talk to different people, "spread your action" they called it. You could never just lie in your bunk and read—that would certainly lead to "negative thinking." I could have killed myself during free time. My mind felt like a jellyfish.

No one has any friends in a drug program. The entire concept is to turn people against one another which is amazingly easy. One of the methods is the encounter group. The people form a circle, and then someone "puts the group" on somebody and people take turns yelling at the person or just talking, sometimes ridiculing, tearing her down, and then the person gets to "deal with the feelings." I tried to get into the spirit of the thing and yell at people and find picky little mistakes in their behavior, but at this I was a glorious failure. Whenever I said something to someone in the group, I soon learned I was just "projecting" my own shit onto them.

One night during the encounter group, Chief edged her way into the circle. The group was on me for vague crimes that people had difficulty articulating. They knew I was up to something but they couldn't figure out what. I hadn't figured it out yet myself.

"You got a letter from one of your beaus, Scarlet," Chief said.

She sat there looking like the cat that ate the canary.

"Some guy named Roy? You know him?"

I nodded. Tall, bony Roy—Vietnam Vet with honey lips, country eyes and a purple heart, inside and out. I felt good but tried to hide it, which isn't easy for me. I'm fine at suppressing misery, but mirth leaks out through my eyeballs at the worst times.

Then she proceeded to read the juicier parts of the letter out loud. It was all full of Roy stuff like he couldn't wait for me to come home and give him "some leg." That sort of thing. I thought, *that Roy*. I was glad he cared enough to write me.

Chief crumpled up the letter. I realized I wasn't ever going to actually get to read it myself.

"You're just a sperm receptacle to him," she said.

I wondered why I was supposed to feel bad that a guy I liked wanted to have sex with me—"bump uglies" as Roy used to say. I thought I'd be feeling a lot worse if he didn't.

It was a strange place, like all drug programs. Not that there weren't enough drug addicts to supply the place, but there weren't enough drug addicts who wanted to give up drugs. So the drug program sent residents to go out and drag people off the streets who weren't drug addicts, but were homeless or nuts or whatever. I figured the state gave them a certain amount of money per resident.

One time the recruiters brought back a girl from Barbados, about 16 with honey-colored skin, owl eyes and black wavy hair. She had tiny bird bones. This girl had never shot drugs in her life, never even smoked pot. But she'd had trouble at home. She said her father was the devil, but she didn't go into detail. She also said she was a virgin. She tried to befriend me when she first got there. But I knew better than to get tight with anyone.

About six other women were in the program at the time. A couple of them were tough black women from the city, one was a 20-something white mother from Long Island, one was a 16-year-old yellow-haired girl, prone to throwing violent temper tantrums and hopelessly in love with one of the male residents.

It's G.I. day and we're cleaning that ramshackle five-story house from top ceiling to bottom step. I'm in the bathroom, down on my hands and knees, scrubbing the crud around the bottom of the toilets. I'm on the last toilet when I hear a loud, terrified horror-movie scream. I jump up and dash into the girls' dorm. The girl from Barbados is shaking. Her bunk is sliced up, pieces of white sheet jutting up through the green blanket like slivers of flesh. A note on her bed says someone is going to kill her. I take her into my arms and hold her as if she is a little child. My eyes won't let go of that shredded blanket on her bed and the pencil written note that calls her a "hor."

A few nights later, I'm awakened by women shrieking. I'm in that groggy deep sleep, the kind that closes over you like a coffin. Voices yell. Pots bang. The noise yanks me out of my sleep, and I raise my head. Shit. Another fire drill? Except that this time there is terror in the voices telling us to, "Get out! Get the hell out!" Curls of smoke snake through the air. I stumble out of bed and follow the others down five flights of steps--thump, thump, thump, thump, thump--until we stand outside in the brittle black night, watching, silent and shivering as the fire trucks pull up. When we go back inside, we're all rounded up into the main room downstairs for a guilt session. The faint stink of smoke embroiders the air around us. Everyone has to sit on the floor, and no one is allowed to talk unless they want to confess. We look around, wondering what it is that we're supposed to admit doing. I notice that the girl from Barbados is not with us but I had seen her outside, weeping silently. We all sit there until Chief arrives and she strides into the room, lips tight as a sealed mason jar. She circles around us, looking at the females with brimstone eyes.

"One of you bitches set fire to her bed," she says. "The whole house is going to stay here until someone cops to the guilt."

But no one would confess. We sat there silently, all twenty of us, on the floor, tired and lost in our own thoughts. Misery had no use for company. Finally, I heard Chief in the hallway with the girl from Barbados. I could see them through the doorway. The girl's beautiful face was smeared with tears.

"The director is going to take you to another facility," Chief told her. "You need to go get your things."

"I'm afraid to go up by myself," the girl told her.

Chief's hands went to her hips. This was all a huge pain in the ass as far as she was concerned, and I knew she'd be glad to get rid of the girl. Chief looked into the room at us. Our eyes met. Then she turned back to the girl.

"Do you trust any of them to go upstairs with you?" she asked.

The girl looked straight at me and pointed a long shaky finger in my direction. I stood up and walked out of the living room. Chief didn't say a word as the two of us went up the steps.

I never saw her again. I suspect the pale blond girl was the one who had been after her. A few days later, she committed some minor infraction of the rules. The level-three residents got all her clothes and threw them out on the sidewalk. Then they dragged her down the hall and shoved her out the door. She landed in the heap of her clothes. She was screaming the whole time, throwing curse words like bricks. It was an awe-inspiring display of fury, something I felt so far removed from that I could only admire it like someone in an airplane flying over an active volcano.

I stood in the office, putting away some filing. No one was around, and the day counselor shut the door and kissed me. His pointed tongue darted in my mouth like he was searching for something. It was the closest I had gotten to feeling good about anything in a long time. I ran my fingers over the crotch of his jeans before I walked out the door and went downstairs for lunch. The rest of the afternoon I felt his eyes nailed to the back of my head while I typed.

That Sunday I was ironing my jeans in a room on the top floor, hearing the music and life of Harlem pulsing like a red heart down in the streets below. Spring had arrived, whistling for the world to come out, come out. But the room enclosed me like the walls of a mausoleum. Sunday was the one day of the week when our lives weren't on a minute-by-minute schedule. On Sundays something stalked me, something enormously large. It felt like someone was sawing through my heart. That night when I went to bed, I knew I couldn't spend another Sunday in that place—not if my life depended on it, which according to them it did.

The next day at lunchtime, I packed my suitcase and became a "splittee". The day counselor had slipped me his address and money for a cab before I left. I found his apartment building and sat on the stoop and waited while New York City strutted by.

"I told them I was sick," he said with a laugh. It didn't seem like a smart move to me, but what did I care? We went upstairs and the first thing I did was take a bath. Then I got into bed with him; sheets of yellow-gray city sunlight pressed up against the window panes unable to get in. The sex was perfunctory, a lead up to what we both wanted.

He went to work for the next two days. I stayed holed up in the apartment and read *Look Homeward, Angel* and cried. Then he got fired.

The next day the gleam in his eye ignited. We went down to the Lower Eastside and copped some of that sweet New York City doogie. We got off in a shooting gallery and I felt like I had plunged off a twenty-story building and landed gently in a warm blue sea. We had to stop every few blocks on the way home, so I could puke.

That afternoon his roommate kicked us out of the apartment and we moved into a room in an old hotel. We didn't have plans. Not much money. And I realized that once the restrictions were gone, I felt absolutely nothing for him—which was a strange thing for me. I should have been delirious: I was in heroin paradise with a dope fiend, who would do anything for me, even lose his job. Could it be I actually loved Roy back in Florida? Or was it just that I loved Florida, or that I missed my worried mother? Now, every day was like Sunday. And I had to find a way to make it stop.

I took a train to Newark to apply for a waitressing job. The owner of the restaurant took a liking to me. I went back that night, worked a shift. It was a Greek restaurant. And the Greek men danced. One of them could have purchased my soul with his black eyes. I wished I wasn't a junkie just that once. I wasn't thinking about my gypsy-faced counselor anymore. I wanted to fall in love with the dancing Greek man, marry him, live in a three-bedroom house in the suburbs and have babies. He had something I wanted but couldn't let myself have. My childhood with my screaming drunk dad and later the silent abyss in my alcoholic stepfather's eyes had taught me that the urge to make a good life with a man was like those covered-up traps you read about in Vietnam, and you were most likely to end up with your heart impaled on a spike if you went after that gilded prize. The restaurant owner rubbed my ass and said he'd see me the next night.

At midnight I got back to the city. I didn't go straight to the hotel but went down to Avenue B by myself. Found the shooting gallery where we'd been a day before. Walked up the dark steps. Knocked on the door.

"It's you again," the man said. I nodded.

Inside the room three or four guys lounged against the walls. No furniture, just the light from the street lamps outside shining in like the glow of the underworld.

"Girl wants some doogie," the man said to one of the others. I handed over my money. I would take some back to the hotel with me, but first I wanted to get off. I got my dope and paid the man two dollars to use the cooker. I borrowed a belt. Someone held it tight for me.

"You got some good veins there for a girl," a voice said. They looked at me from far away, waiting for me to arrive. The needle bit me and then nestled into my vein. Such a clean hit running through me like the Orient Express. New York heroin is like a daddy holding you, kissing you on the neck. New York heroin turns you into an angel. It's white, not dark and red like the Mexican heroin that I shot back home. It's as close to death as you could want to come with your eyes open. It tasted like the sweet breath of Buddha.

The next morning, I was groggy and sleepish, someone knocking on the door of the hotel room. My fellow fugitive lay next to me. We were friendly because we still had some stuff in our systems. He got up and answered the door. Then before I could do anything my brother was standing in the room. I could see by the plastered look of rationality on his face that he wanted to kick this guy's ass. Like it was his fault. Which it wasn't. I was the bloodless femme fatale, the vampire girl. And he looked at me with the cover up to my chin.

"What?" I asked. "What? What? What?"

"You have to go back to the drug program," he said.

"Shit," I said.

But my brother was looking at me with his green-brown eyes—the same brother who tried to be a father to me when he was fifteen and I was four. The same brother who took me horseback riding, who taught me how to canoe, how to bowl, how to count to ten in German. This hard look settled in his eyes, and his jaw was set. And I became a small child heading back to my bedroom because I'd been bad again.

"All right," I said. The former day counselor stared at me in disbelief. My brother turned around and walked out of the room.

When I went back to the program, I was put on a work contract—probably an eternal one. My sin had been unforgivable. I had taken down one of the rescued ones. The work contract meant I wore a stocking cap and worked from 6 a.m. until midnight and nobody ever spoke to me.

I didn't mind the contract so much. At least people left me alone. But then one morning the smell of vinegar which we used to clean the big stove made me retch till my guts ached. I had to go to bed. I was yellow all over, and my piss was dark. Hepatitis. I stayed in a bed in a room by myself and couldn't leave. No one talked to me. When they brought food up to me, they set it down on the floor and wouldn't even look at me. At least no one set fire to my bed.

After a week, they sent me to a doctor to see if I was over the hepatitis. They sent my old reliable escort with me—a tall, thin dude who didn't like white chicks anyway. They weren't trusting me with anyone who might be susceptible to my vortex of destruction. We took the subway to the doctor's office. As we rode through the dark tunnels staring ahead and swaying like zombies, I kept thinking how Manhattan was like Alcatraz. I didn't have a clue how to get off the damn thing. There sure as hell wasn't any subway line to Florida.

The doctor looked at my eyes, made me piss in a cup, jabbed me with a giant needle and sucked out all but a few drops of blood.

"You're O.K.," he said. "You can go back to work."

He wrote something on a piece of paper and gave it to my escort. The guy smiled for the first time since I'd known him.

We walked outside the doctor's office. As we headed toward the subway, I saw a green sign about a block away. I stopped and squinted my eyes to read it. My heart rolled over like an engine when you turn on the ignition.

"Come on," he said.

"No," I said. "I'm not going back."

"What? Don't do this to me," he said.

"I'm so sorry," I smiled at him. What a dishonor this would be for him. I started walking and went right past the subway entrance straight for that sign—"95 South" with a little arrow pointing down the adjoining street. I turned the corner and headed for the interstate. It was only a few blocks away!

When I got there, I stuck out my thumb and I was gone.

This guy in a black Peterbilt semi-truck picked me up in Jersey. He was short, fat and red-faced, hunched over the wheel. He was a talker and he wanted to know everything about me. Like I really wanted to talk about my glamorous life. But you know, you're riding in somebody's truck, you got to pay for the ride one way or another. So I told him about being in the drug program, about not being sure what I would do once I got back to Florida. I didn't tell him how the people at that place had told me my mom said she didn't want me back. It didn't sound like something she'd say, but I didn't know anything anymore.

"I'll get you an apartment," the truck driver said to me.

"Well, that's O.K. I'll get by," I said.

"No, I mean it," he said. "I'll take care of you."

He was doing speed, he said. He didn't offer me any. God, I was tired.

It was night. The highway thrummed below the steadily rolling wheels. I was shutting down everything I had been through in New York, closing it up, turning off the lights.

"Go back in the cab and get some sleep," he said. "I won't bother you. I promise."

"No thanks," I said.

"Go on," he said, his voice friendly, cajoling. I was so tired. Still feeling the after-effects of the hepatitis. And my mind wasn't working right. All my instincts were shut down. Finally, I crawled up into the cab where it was warm and dark as a womb and fell asleep as soon as I closed my eyes.

Then it was later, and the truck was pulled off the road.

He held a meaty, gristled fist in my face. I was cornered in the dark cab of the truck. The thick air smelled like something wet and rotting.

"I'll beat the shit out of you," he said. His dark voice moved through me like absolute zero. "Just do what I tell you to do."

His pants were open and his little frog penis edged toward my mouth. My Judas body did everything he told it to do. Then he fell asleep, his body like a wall between me and the door. I tried not to, but I drifted off. When I woke up, we were going south at 80 miles an hour. I slid back into the passenger seat and stared out the window. We were in a green tunnel.

We pulled into the north end of Jacksonville. I smelled the paper mill at the county line. I tried not to think about the night before. Instead I kept remembering the day counselor from the drug program and the way he'd been standing in the shabby lobby of the old hotel, saying, "I can't believe you're doing this" as I walked away.

The truck driver hadn't stopped again, but the interstate was closed for a couple of miles and he had to take old Highway One. Jacksonville is a large city; it spreads out like an oil spill. In my mind I practiced saying, "you can let me out here" because as soon as we got across the river, I'd be close to my mom's. But I looked over at him, and even though he'd been the one jamming his dick into my face, he was mad as murder.

"What're you looking at?" he said.

I didn't answer him, just turned my head and tried to gauge the distance to the ground. Hell, I thought, I'm going to die. I saw a vision of myself, my throat blue and mottled, my naked body twisted and rotting in some leaves somewhere no one would find me. Wouldn't the world be just a bit better off? I thought of all the people I'd screwed over—the day counselor, my brother, my mother, myself, countless others.

"I'm gonna make you do it again," he said and stared hard at me to see just what the hell I was gonna do about it. I felt as if I was sealed in concrete. I tried to remember if I'd ever done anything decent in my entire life. I suddenly remembered the smell of burned mattress, and the soft hand of the girl from Barbados on my arm that night as I helped her pack her things and her lilting voice as she said, "Thank you." I took a deep breath.

A few minutes later, the truck driver came to a stoplight, and there was a highway patrol car in the next lane. I jerked the handle of the cab and flung the door open. As I dropped to the road, the truck driver's eyes grew wide and his little mouth went round and dark like a gun barrel. I slammed the door shut and ran to the sidewalk. The light turned green, and he ground the gears and took off.

I turned around, my fists in tight balls. What I felt was a scream but it came out like more of a laugh. I closed my eyes and took a deep breath. I couldn't believe I was alive. And I was home.

When I opened my eyes again, the highway patrol car was gone. Across the street, a live oak tree in an empty lot spread its branches outward, dripping Spanish moss. The warm southern sunlight spread before me like a welcome mat.

Summertime

I headed toward an old gas station on the corner where I found a payphone. The heat wrapped its arms around me.

It took Roy about twenty minutes to get to where I was, sitting on the stoop outside the gas station. The black man who ran the gas station had bought me a Nehi grape soda, and I was enjoying every drop. Roy's smile was a rainbow, and I laughed as I slowly got up and strolled over to him.

"How ya doin?" he asked like I hadn't been gone at all.

"Not bad," I said, leaning against the door, my face in the open window.

“Your girl is gone,” he said.

“My girl?”

“Angie,” he said, inhaling deeply on a Marlboro.

“What do you mean, gone?” I asked.

“She ate a bottle of quaaludes and drank a quart of vodka.”

At that moment, it felt like the blood had evaporated from my body. She was my only friend. My only fucking friend and now she was gone.

I spent the first week, lounging by the pool at the apartment complex. I wrote my mom who was in North Carolina where she had a summer job and told her I had come home. There were some letters for me from Charlie, but I didn't open them.

My car, a Cutlass skylark that I'd gotten for four hundred dollars a few months before I left for New York, still ran perfectly. I got a job, modeling lingerie at a restaurant during lunchtime. It was sleazy and the money wasn't even good, but I got free lunch.

Soon after I got home, I went to the dock down by the river and watched the small waves jostle each other. I felt threads inside me slowly unraveling, loosening, breaking. They'd been frayed for a long time, ever since I was a child, I suppose. Someone inside me who had the capacity to feel enormous pain just drifted away. I had quite a talent, I realized, quite a talent for shunning the darkness.

I thought about Angie. What bothered me was that I would never see her again. And I wanted to. I wanted to be able to call her up, to go to the beach with her, to go shopping, to do all the things we had never done. I was living in a movie that someone else had written. I gazed at the oblivious blue sky above me, and I wondered when it would be over, when I could walk off the set and assume a new role. The river moaned, and in the distance I could see rain falling, heading toward me. I lay down on the dock, the water flowing by like long dark hair. The rain came closer. The river slowed its chop chopping. Everything stopped. I felt immobile like a figure in an oil painting. Then the rain fell softly and the river water was docile under the pricking drops. I got up and went inside. I thought I might read some poetry. I got out my book of T.S. Eliot, but I couldn't read it. The words lay cold and blue under my eyes.

The phone rang. I picked it up, half thinking it would be her. That it was a mistake.

"Hey, doll," Roy said.

"Hey, yourself," I said.

"What's wrong?" he asked. I couldn't tell him. He listened to my silence.

Then he said, "I got fitty dollars, but my transmission is busted. Can you give me a ride downtown to cop?"

I hung up, grabbed my car keys and walked outside.

Another One Bites the Dust

I spent the rest of the summer hanging out with Roy and Hank. Sometimes I'd go out with just one of them—usually whichever one happened to answer the phone. One night I went over to pick up Roy, and Hank got in the car and said Roy had gone somewhere else.

"Really?" I asked.

"Yeah, he went to cop for some guys," Hank said. It was only later that I found out that Roy had still been in the shower. In some ways, at first, they seemed kind of interchangeable to me.

One time the three of us went down to the hole—an area in the black part of town—to cop some heroin. I was riding up in the front between the two of them, and this guy who's selling us the dope leans in the car, points at me and says, "Which one of y'all does she belong to?"

"Neither," I answered. "They belong to me."

One night Roy and Hank and I headed over to an apartment in Riverside. We'd already hit a doctor for a scrip and gotten some Dilaudids, and Hank figured we could sell them there; besides he was sweet on the girl who lived in the apartment which was just down the street from my high school in a brick quadruplex.

When we got out of the car, I stood for a minute, looking down the street at the school. My high school was one of the first ones ever built in Jacksonville. A statue of Robert E. Lee stood in the front. It was an old sand-stone colored brick building and I had few good memories of the place, but still I knew I had only gone down since those days. I'd been out of high school for three years and in that time, I'd been married, lost my husband to prison, gone to California and lost my boyfriend to another prison, bounced in and out of a drug program, and perhaps helped drive my best friend to suicide.

"Whatcha thinking about?" Roy asked me, and looked down into my eyes. His own were big and coffee-colored.

"Nothin'," I said. We went upstairs into the apartment.

We met Hank's new chick, and I didn't like her much. She was about 18 but seemed to me like she'd gotten stuck around thirteen, kind of baby-faced and stupid. I looked around the apartment, just your regular bland Jacksonville atmosphere, Goodwill furniture, but nice hardwood floors, open windows with fans stirring up the hot air. Frogs made night noises outside. It had an old smell. All those places do.

I sat down on the couch and crossed my legs. I was wearing jeans and a pair of leather sandals. Every year my mom and I would go down to St. Augustine and buy leather sandals from the same guy. These were last year's model.

It's been a long, hard year, I was thinking when I heard someone say in that typical fake southern oh-so-friendly way, "Why, Trish, how are you doing?"

I looked up and there was Cynthia, Timothy's wife, who I hadn't seen since I left them in California. She acted like we were old buds.

"I'm all right. How about you?"

"Fine," she said and sat down beside me, all eager to talk. I saw that it wasn't totally an act. People are like that. They could hate your guts for years and then suddenly it's as if they've hated you so long that you become a part of their lives. So she tossed her long hair behind her shoulder and leaned in close.

"How long have you been back?" I asked.

""Since before Christmas," she said. "Timothy and I came back after Big Steve got busted. Timothy's clean. He got a job working for his Dad."

I looked at her skeptically.

"I swear it," she said.

"Y'all still together?" I asked.

She shrugged her shoulders and looked at her fingernails and scraped off a pink fleck of polish.

"No," she said. "I'm going out with someone else now. I'm over Timothy. But I still see him sometimes. He was really torn up about Big Steve."

Roy and Hank came in from the kitchen where they'd made themselves something to eat.

"Want a sandwich, baby?" Roy asked.

I shook my head and turned back to Cynthia.

"What do you mean he was torn up about Big Steve? He only got a few months for parole violation. He's probably out by now," I said. I didn't know what to trust coming from Cynthia. She had a flair for the dramatic.

Her eyes grew wide and she leaned back away from me, looking at me as if I'd grown an extra arm. Then her eyebrows squeezed together.

"Oh shit," she said. "You don't know, do you?"

An icy feeling snaked down my throat.

"Big Steve died a week after he got out of prison. He overdosed. Timothy thinks someone gave him a hot shot," she said.

The cold settled in my belly. I couldn't feel a thing, but in my head I heard that voice say, "That's two."

"Damn," Hank said. Roy studied me from the chair across the room. I looked up at him. His dark eyes were sympathetic and warm. They were like molasses.

"Well, I thought for sure you knew, Trish. There was a funeral and everything," Cynthia was saying.

I looked at her.

"Nobody gave Big Steve a hot shot," I said. Cynthia looked at me strangely, but I couldn't say anything else. I had to get out of there. The air had grown cotton thick, and it was impossible to breathe.

Roy and I left.

I couldn't stop thinking about Big Steve. Just like Angie, I thought. And I thought about his mom, about Angie's mom, Charlie's mom, Roy's mom and my mom, too. They hadn't done anything to deserve what we had given them. A bad, black feeling wrapped its hands around my throat.

Then I remembered Big Steve singing country music and laughing that sweet rolling chuckle of his. I remembered his Buddhism and wondered what he could come back as. I hoped it would be as a dolphin or a blue heron, something free.

Roy and I got in his car. The night air was warm and cotton-soft on the skin. As he drove over the bridge crossing the St. John's, I looked at the sad, old city—a smattering of lights, buildings struggling to stay up, memories that toppled over on each other. Roy ran through the toll booth without paying. The little alarm rang futilely.

"Let's move, Roy," I said.

"Where to?" he asked.

I saw a sign that said 95 South. The West had killed Big Steve, and the North had killed something in me, but 95 South was the River Jordan.

"Miami," I said.

Best Friend

Tall Australian pines sprouted along the side of I-95, south of Palm Beach. The road seemed to go on forever and ever, chopped by mile markers and exit signs. Roy sat at the wheel. Roy was like a boat captain at his leisure, smoking his Marlboro, his arm resting on the steering wheel.

Neither of us had been this far south before. We came into the outskirts of the city and it looked ordinary, exits to numbered streets, gas stations, low buildings crowded up next to the interstate. Suddenly we came over a rise in the highway and both of us gasped.

The city lay before us, dazzling in the sunset. Oz had nothing on this place. I'd never seen anything like it before. Highways intersected in graceful curves, glass buildings caught the sunlight and turned it into colors. Against the horizon stood red and blue buildings with odd holes in them where the sky glowed through.

"I like it here," I told Roy. Roy flashed his wide smile. Then he reached over and shook my knee.

"Welcome home, doll," he said.

We came to Miami under the pretext that I would attend college, and in fact, I was registered and did go to classes. We got an apartment in a one-story building near the university. We had palm trees in our front yard, Naugahyde-covered furniture in the living room, and jalousied windows in our doors.

Roy and I got on the methadone program in order to meet some other junkies and find out where to cop. We stayed on a low dose so we could get off of it as soon as possible. It's not that methadone isn't a good high, but it's a controlled high. The ups and the downs evaporate. Roy had a hard time peeing on command, and they'd threatened to cut him off if he couldn't come up with a clean urine drop.

After the morning trip to the clinic, we'd stop for pancakes at the Sambo's restaurant in classy Coral Gables. We'd watch the rich people chop chop down Miracle Mile, diving from their Mercedes Benzes and Rolls Royces into the bright heat and then into the cool stores.

In the afternoons I went to my classes. The methadone combined with the lectures made me drowsy. My head would slump to my desk and the garbled words of professors dribbled into my ears like liquid. But I managed to do all right.

After my presentation in the oral interpretation class, the professor called me to come speak to her. Everyone else filed out. My tongue roved around my dry mouth trying to loosen itself. I blinked at her.

"How do you do it?" she asked. "You sit there and sleep through the entire class day after day and then when it comes time for your performance you stand here and deliver something that is absolutely flawless. How do you do it?"

She had black hair, a thin, pensive face, inquisitive eyes made large by her tortoise shell glasses. I didn't want her peering into me with all those questions of hers. I shrugged my shoulders. What could I say?

The junkies at the methadone clinic were all closed-mouthed and unfriendly as a gathering of cockroaches. Roy and I gave up on them. Finally, we overheard someone mention the good dope that could be found in a little town called Perrine down in south Dade. So we took a drive down there one day. Roy's favorite band was Queen and on the radio, we heard them singing "You're my best friend." Roy squeezed my hand. We found the main drag: unpainted one-story buildings and vacant lots. A man—dark brown skin, wiry energetic frame, walked quickly along the street. Gradually he seemed to sense someone watching him. He turned around and saw us. He looked at us for a minute and then smiled ever so slightly. We stopped the car and rolled down the window. Here was our new best friend.

Keep Your Hands Off My Stack

Roy and I got glassy-eyed and greedy from living around all that money. Jaguars, Porsches, Rolls, Bentleys. One time I test drove a baby blue Mercedes Benz. I would have done anything to get the car. Anything except give up dope, but we'd already gone through all the money I had for living expenses.

"I gotta get some work," I told Roy one morning when we sat at the dinette in our squalid little apartment, drinking instant coffee. "We need to get some of this money down here."

Roy agreed, and we both knew he was not going to make the kind of money we wanted by delivering appliances, which is the only job he'd ever had. We'd also gotten kicked off the methadone program for having dirty urine.

"Think I'll check out that place on Dixie Highway," I said. He knew exactly what I was talking about: a big square building with no windows. A sign outside advertised exotic dancers. We'd driven by it, and it had lodged in our consciousness.

"I hear them girls make as much as a hundred bucks a night," Roy said.

"It's not like it's prostitution," I said.

"You want me to drive you?" he asked.

I shook my head. I needed to do this alone.

That afternoon about four o'clock, I drove down to the Cheetah Lounge. I wore lipstick, dark brown eye shadow and mascara. I looked in the rearview mirror. I didn't look very exotic, but I had to give it a shot.

So I went in. The place was dark and pungent with the sour smell of distilled spirits. Disco music bounced from the black walls. A big horseshoe bar occupied the center of the room with a few dusty old men seated by themselves, nursing glasses of dark liquid. On a stage at the far end of the room, a girl wearing a G-string swung her hips back and forth not quite to the beat of the music. The bartender, a woman in her thirties, noticed me standing there, staring.

"Can I help you?" she asked.

"I was wondering if there were any job openings?" I said.

She turned her back on me, and I wasn't sure what that meant until a few moments later, an enormously fat man came over and introduced himself as Sam.

"Come on back," he said and started walking toward the back of the room. He didn't say he was the manager or anything, but I followed him into a dressing room kind of place. A harsh fluorescent light glared down on women's clothes scattered on chairs. The floor was covered by the grimiest carpet I'd ever seen. Piles of high heels were jumbled under the counters. Square mirrors with gold patterns on them had been stuck to the walls.

"You ever dance before?" the man asked.

"Yes," I lied. "At a bar in Jacksonville."

"All right. Let's see what you look like," he said. I stared at him.

"Go ahead. Strip," he said.

I didn't know if I was supposed to turn it into an act or just take off my clothes. For some reason, I had dressed as if I were applying for a real job somewhere, a secretarial job or something. I decided simply to get undressed without any fanfare, taking off my pumps, my blouse, my skirt, my bra, then my pantyhose. But since the dancers were only topless, I left on my white bikini panties.

"Stick some of those high heels on," he said.

I looked through the jumble of high heels under the counter and found a pair of red platforms. I slipped them on and stood up.

"I feel like the Leaning Tower of Pisa," I said.

"The what?" he asked.

"Nothing," I answered.

"Then shut up and turn around," he said in a matter of fact tone. I didn't take it personally. None of this seemed to be personal. I was showing him the merchandise. It felt strange, but after what I'd learned how to shut off my feelings like a light switch.

I glanced around at the walls. There were cracks in them and water stains. This was a room which had never heard a kind word.

"Stop at the bar and tell Sylvia I just hired you. She'll tell you your schedule," he said. Then he got up and walked out while I put on my clothes. I stuck the red shoes in my pocketbook.

I went back into the dim bar. The girl who had been dancing on the stage now stood on top of a table and gyrated above the face of an enraptured businessman. My god, I thought, it's so easy. Show your tits, wave your crotch at them and they're hypnotized. I sat down at the bar. Sylvia came over to me. She wore bright blue eye shadow and orange lipstick.

"Can I get something to drink?" I asked.

"Five dollars," she said.

"All I want is a coke," I said. "He's hiring me. I need to know my schedule."

"He didn't make you give him a blow job, did he?" she asked.

I shook my head. I didn't think she believed me. She poured me a coke and said she'd be back in a minute. She had to wait on some customers on the other side of the bar. I drank my coke and let my eyes drift over to the dancing girl. I paid attention to her, taking notes. Her movements were languorous as if she were dancing in her sleep.

"You work here?" a voice asked me.

A dark-haired guy sat two seats away. He was young, maybe about Roy's age or even younger.

"Not yet," I said.

"You look like a secretary," he said as if it was the highest compliment he could pay me. He had a Cuban accent, and he was beautiful.

Sylvia came back over with a sheet of paper.

"You can start tonight if you want," she said. "Nine o'clock."

"All right," I said.

"What's your name?" she asked.

"Trish," I said.

"Trish? That's no name for a dancer," Sylvia said. She studied me and then said, "Your name will be Cinnamon."

She wrote the name on the sheet of paper and then walked away again.

"That's a stupid name," the Cuban guy said. "Trish is much nicer."

I shrugged. He stood up, and I glanced over as he pulled out his money clip to pay for his drink. Even in the dark, I could see the hundred dollar bills he rifled through. Finally, he threw down a twenty.

"Keep the change," he called out to her. The light from outside flashed across the desolate faces of the other customers as he walked out of the door. His presence had unnerved me. I felt a hollowness inside my chest. I finished the coke and gathered my purse. At least I could tell Roy I had a job.

I stepped outside and let my eyes adjust to the light. As I walked to my car, I noticed a white Porsche with the engine running. The Cuban guy rolled down his window.

"Want to go to the beach?" he asked. I stared at him for a moment. Traffic roared by. The air was hot and sticky. Something about him looked cool and sweet.

"I'd like some ice cream," I said.

"Chocolate or vanilla?" he asked.

Riding That Train

I never went back to the Cheetah.

The Cuban guy's name was Paolo, and he was an honest-to-god genuine dope smuggler, who loved everything American including Frank Sinatra. We'd ride down to the beach in his Porsche, singing "New York, New York." He told people I was his secretary. He told me that he'd been sent to America by his parents when he was fifteen. He'd had to stay in foster homes until he turned eighteen.

"Castro, he drafts you into his army when you turn fifteen. My mama didn't want me to go," he said. "And my papi is in the underground. Someday we'll overthrow that bastard. Get all my uncles out of prison."

Paolo's English had a lot of gaps in it. It didn't matter, we didn't do much talking. Sometimes he took me to one of the restaurants on Calle Ocho, and we ate black beans and arroz con pollo and plantains. We had sex in motels and hotels all over Miami from little rundown places off Tamiami Trail to the big ocean-huggers along Miami Beach. I told Roy I thought he was trying to fuck America itself.

Every time I left Paolo, I had two or three hundred dollars in my wallet and a baggie full of cocaine. Sometimes he also gave me a baggie of reefer for Roy. He and Roy never met, but they had a mutual respect for each other.

In Miami, we keep the blinds closed all day, watch "Andy of Mayberry" reruns, and guffaw at the "Beverly Hillbillies." The Hungry Jack biscuit commercial comes on, and a southern woman calls out, "Hongry! Hongry Jack!"

"That's you, Hank," I say when the big foot of Hungry Jack appears in the frame.

Hank is on one side of me in the big bed and Roy is on the other. Hank rolls over laughing. Our white cat, Stinky, sleeps on top of the television. Roy gets up to make us all some ditty-wa, which is what the Wiggins boys call coffee. We drink Maxwell instant.

"Anybody want any breakfast?" I ask.

Roy lights his first cigarette of the morning. He waits for a moment.

"A breakfast fix," he says and then smiles in that disarming way of his. It is a contest to see who can go the longest without mentioning the need for heroin. Roy always loses. I groan, roll over, feel Roy's hand in my hair.

"I love you," he whispers in my ear.

"Find my jeans, will you? Hank, I got enough money for me and Roy. You got any money?" I mutter, my face pressed against the pillow.

Hank says no, so I gotta get him high, too.

Roy drives. I ride shotgun. And Hank rides in the back. In Perrine we visit our friend. We visit him as often as we can. We get high in his house, learn the names of all six of his children, eat ribs with him and his wife, laugh with him, watch his television set. This is our life, our Miami life. Mostly it is just me and Roy. But sometimes Hank comes down to stay with us until I send him back home to Jacksonville, sometimes a long-distance truck driving friend of Roy's visits. Other sundry visitors arrive—our country cousins.

In Miami, I grow skinny. I'd put on weight in the New York drug program, but here I am rail-thin, my skin like cheap cloth on metal rods. I can float wherever I want to go. I paint my nails radical red. I think of myself as a dragonfly. This is the way the world wants its women, I think, sharp-boned and ready to break.

Two o'clock in the morning, Paolo would call me, say, "Come over to the Fontainebleau. I'm lonely. You can type up some letters."

I'd kiss Roy and then roll out of bed, get dressed in something basic, something black and dab on some lipstick—no eye make-up or blush. Paolo couldn't stand a whorish look.

"You want me to drive you?" Roy would ask.

I'd shake my head, promise to bring something home for him and head out the door into the warm, slippery night.

Most of these times it would just be me and Paolo, snorting fat crystalline lines, talking some and then always the sex just before dawn, something to help him go to sleep. Then I 'd take home my cocaine for the night. Roy and I would stay up shooting it, our eyes getting wild, our arms covered with blood. The oily nights damp with sweat that coated our bodies like wax. Blood spray made little red tracks on the yellow walls from where we cleaned out the needles

Some nights, Paolo might have business partners over, and he'd ask me to bring along some girls. I found a few girls at the college who liked to party. So I'd bring them, and there we'd all be: thin glassy girls ages 19 to 22 and gold-braceleted men ages 24 to 30 in various stages of undress in the living room of an apartment.

The room is bland—furnished in contemporary rent-a-couch beige. On the coffee table is a bowl full of white Quaaludes. A mirror is passed around, set down, couples disappear into bedrooms and later the girls return, drawn to the mirror, the hundred dollar bill that fits snugly in their nostril. It is here that I can see us as we truly are—vultures, parasites, tapeworms. We can barely keep up the pretense of smiling, as we diligently frazzle our brain cells. I wonder occasionally if we would do this sort of thing if we did not have the drugs, would we gather simply to exhibit ourselves, to have our bodies admired, to revel in our lusts. But I cannot know. All I know is that we had cut loose the excesses of personality. The men reduced us to our tits and our cunts, and we reduced them to their wallets and their vials.

Coming Back to Me

"Jasper Collins," I said. Jasper and Hank were sitting in the living room, eating the last of my powdered donuts and drinking my Pepsi.

"Jasper gave me a ride down, honey," Hank said. "Come here and squeeze my neck."

I hugged Hank and he kissed me on the lips.

"You look good, Trish," Jasper said. "How are things going?"

Roy came in, wearing his boxer shorts.

"Look who's here, doll," he said.

"Yes, I see them," I said. I put my books down on the table and went into the bedroom, shutting the door behind me. I stripped down to my slip and crawled under the covers. Hank came in a few minutes later.

"You don't seem happy to see me," he said, sitting on the bed.

"Aw, Hank, it's just that I can't support every swinging dick who comes here from Jacksonville," I said. He lay down beside me and put his head on my shoulder.

"We won't stay long," he said.

"Promise?" I asked.

"Promise," he said. Then his hand reached between my legs. I hadn't had sex with Hank in a million years, and then only twice, but I didn't stop him as he shucked his clothes and slid in between my legs. I 'd begun to feel like a dinner buffet. It was over in a second or two because dope fiends are extremely sensitive when there's no dope in their bloodstream.

Roy didn't look up when I came out of the bedroom and went into the bathroom to clean up.

Later that night I went out with Paolo and came home about three in the morning. I came in the back door. All three of them—Roy, Hank and Jasper—were sitting at the dinette table in the kitchen waiting for me. They reminded me of baby birds, looking at me expectantly, beaks agape.

"I'm tired," I said. "I'm going to bed."

A shadow of disappointment crossed their faces. Roy stood up and kissed the top of my head.

"He didn't give you nothing?" he asked.

"No," I said, "Except this." Then I pulled out a quarter o-z of white glittering powder.

"Shit," Jasper whispered. He gazed at the cocaine and then at me with wonder in his eyes. Then he said, "I wish I was a fucking chick."

Hank laughed. "I'm sure they's some old boys who would help you find out what it's like."

"Fuck you," Jasper said.

We all went into the bedroom, got out our works and went straight to business—poking holes in the thin sheets of skin, missing the veins sometimes, other times getting the target, sitting back down, listening to our ears scream, trying to catch our breaths as they slipped into the funnel above us. It was good coke, but even the best gets less and less meaningful the more you do it. We still had plenty left when dawn broke, but we were wired as hell. I thought about putting the cocaine up and saving some for later, maybe selling some. An impossible dream unless we could come down.

"Man, what's that smell?" Roy asked. We all looked around. Something smelled like shit.

Finally, Jasper said, "It's me."

"What the hell, Jasper?" Hank said. "Did you shit on yourself?"

Jasper nodded. He looked ghastly with his bloody arms and his wide spiraling eyeballs.

"Well, go wash off, Jasper," I told him.

"I'm not leaving," he said.

"You better go in that bathroom," I said. I had lost all patience. The cocaine had sizzled every nerve in my body.

"Don't shoot anymore," he said.

"It's not your coke, weasel," I said. "Go clean off. Now."

He did finally.

We had to cop some heroin or the cocaine would kill us, so Roy and I went down to Perrine and traded some of the coke. We deliberately took our time getting back to Hank and Jasper. Before we got home, we stopped at the supermarket and bought a package of disposable diapers to give to Jasper. Roy and I figured our lives weren't too bad, not too bad at all. I should have known that Jasper was an omen for disaster coming down the road.

Sure enough, a couple of weeks after they left, there came a knock on the door. I opened it, and there stood Charlie.

"Charlie," I said.

"Hey, baby," he said back. "You gonna invite me in?"

"Who is it, doll?" Roy called from the bedroom.

I just stared at Charlie. Then I finally found my voice.

"It's Charlie," I called to Roy. I stood aside and Charlie came in.

"How'd you know where I live?" I asked.

"A little bird named Jasper," he said and grinned at me.

Roy came out of the bedroom. He wasn't wearing a shirt and you could see how scrawny he was.

"Hey, man," he said to Charlie and they shook hands. "When did you get out?"

Charlie's arms were all muscled up the way guys are whenever they get out of the joint. It'd been what, two and a half years?, since I watched him walk through that door of the courthouse, and a year and a half since I visited him.

"A few weeks ago. Came down to see my wife," Charlie said and smiled.

"Ex-wife," I told him. "Ex."

Charlie shrugged.

"Well, have a seat," Roy said. Roy had been lonely, and he'd gotten so used to the idea of me fucking another guy that Charlie's presence didn't bother him. He was glad to have someone from home to talk to.

"Y'all got a nice crib here," Charlie said, looking around, settling himself down on the couch in the living room. "Real Florida, terrazzo floors, jalousied windows, sand spurs in the yard."

"Yeah," Roy said. "We've had just about every swinging dick from home come visit us so far. Hard to get rid of them." He was laughing and saying this mainly for my benefit because he knew I got sick of all the visitors.

"So how are your classes going?" Charlie asked me.

"Great," Roy answered for me. "She made the dean's list the first semester."

Charlie looked at my pile of books and then over at me. I was sure he wondered how I managed school and juggled my career as a junkie.

"We got back on the methadone maintenance program a month or so ago," I told him.

"You all aren't shooting dope?" Charlie asked, looking at the fresh track marks on my arm.

"Sometimes. But not every day," I answered.

"We've been getting a lot of coke," Roy told him. "The shit down here is pure as rain water."

Charlie didn't ask where we get this coke from. He didn't say anything about how we survived, but I could see in his eyes the judgment.

"You working?" Charlie asked Roy.

"No," he said, puckering up his lips.

"He had a job, but he got hives," I interjected with a new and sudden feeling of disgust. All along I'd loved Roy, loved him like I loved my breath, like I loved the sweet dope that we bought in Perrine. But now I saw him through Charlie's eyes—the kept man of a working girl, a docile pimp.

It was not entirely true that Roy didn't not work. For one thing he took care of me. He drove me wherever I need to go. He made sure I ate. He loved me, he bathed me. I was a full time job. He was the sentinel against my loneliness. Everyone who visited us knew about Paolo. Everyone knew this, and everyone up until that moment had thought what a great enterprise we were embarked upon. Everyone up until Charlie walked in the door of the house. He never said a word about it, just met my eyes with a long hard gaze when Roy wasn't looking, and I knew what he was thinking. For the first time, I felt the shame of it all.

Charlie bought food for the apartment and paid for the gas in my car. Like some sort of blind man, Roy didn't see the game that was being played here. He was still back in the country where everyone cheats each other honestly.

One night craziness sails in on the wind. It's near the end of the spring semester. The frogs chirp madly outside. I have final exams coming up. I have been kicked out of one of the honor clubs at school for being a fuck up. I am sitting on the big king-sized bed in my bedroom reading the Norton Anthology of Literature. Charlie and Roy are in the living room.

"Do you mind if we come in and watch some TV?" Roy asks. Without a word, I throw the Norton Anthology of English Literature, Volume One, at him and hit him square in the chest.

"Damn it," I scream at him. I have never screamed at him before. I have never even been mad at him, not even when he forged my name on some checks when we were trying to kick one time. I have never, ever cursed at him.

He stands there as if I am suddenly speaking in tongues, and he watches me whirl out of the house. Then he follows me outside. We sit in the Impala.

"What's wrong?" he asks.

"I don't know," I tell him. "Maybe you should go home for awhile."

"I don't want to go home," he says.

I look up. Just then I see a tall black man walk up to our neighbor's back door. Our neighbor is a white woman, pretty much mono-racial in her relationships as far as we've been able to tell.

"Who do you suppose that is?" I ask.

The man walks around to the front of the building. Roy shrugs.

"Do you think that was someone who knows us? Somebody looking for us?" I ask. "One of the Perrine dudes?"

Roy and I go back inside.

Charlie looks up from the book he's reading, *The Detective*.

"There's somebody out there," Roy says. I go out front to look but I don't see anything. Then I go to the back door. I'm holding a glass of Kool-Aid in my hand. Stinky is meowing and following me, begging for food. I open the back door and see the tall man again.

"Are you looking for somebody?" I ask.

In a second, he has pulled his T-shirt over his face and in the next second he has grabbed me by the arm.

"Yeah, you," he says. My Kool-Aid flies across the room, and the cat skitters away so fast she breaks the sound barrier. And then Roy, who has picked up a large bat, swats the guy in the head. The guy instantly lets go of me and runs back down the pebble driveway with Roy and Charlie running after him. Roy and Charlie never catch the guy, but the police come and say he was an escapee from the South Florida Mental Hospital. I remember my own craziness from earlier when I threw the book at Roy. Maybe we were all escapees of some sort.

Charlie leaves for Jacksonville the next day. I have four blue bruises on my arm from the man's grip that do not fade for a week.

One night about eight o'clock, the phone rings.

"Hello, Princess," Paolo's soft voice sort of murmurs. "Can you come out tonight?"

I'm thinking about Charlie, the way he stared into my eyes before he left like he was looking way down an alley and trying to see what was there.

Roy raises his eyebrows at me. He's hoping it's Paolo on the phone.

"Yeah," I tell him. "I can come over. Where are you?"

"The Fontainebleau," he says. "I just got back."

I don't ask from where.

After I hang up, I take my time getting dressed. Roy studies me. He can read my moods and he knows I don't want to go.

"You can stay home if you want to," he says, but he really hopes I'll go.

"We gotta pay rent, Roy," I tell him. "Who's gonna do that? You?"

I walk out the door, hairbrush in my hand, and get in the car. There's no valet at the door for some reason so I park in the lot near the hotel and walk. A breeze blows off the ocean and for a moment I forget about everything and just feel good. Funny how that can happen.

I take my time going to his room. I like Paolo. He's handsome and gentle. He's young. He's into some kind of shit, but he's not Al Capone. I guess Charlie has just gotten under my skin. I don't know if I ever really loved Charlie, but somehow I always felt as if I belonged to him. I should have stood by him when he went to prison but that's not the kind of person I am. He knew that. Hell, I was only 18.

I go down the long hallway and knock on the door to Paolo's room. No one answers. A couple of Japanese businessmen pass me on their way to the elevator. I stare at the door, go into my little Gucci bag that Paolo bought for me and look at the number I had scrawled onto a piece of paper. I knock again. Then I reach down and turn the doorknob. It's unlocked.

"Paolo?" I call into the room. I enter slowly. The room has two beds, one of them looks slept in. Outside the night nuzzles against the windows. The television is on: Channel Ten News with that blond-haired lady. I stick my head in the bathroom.

Paolo lies on the tile floor, eyes open, unblinking, blood pooling around his head. He doesn't move, and there is no rise and fall to his chest. He looks like a puppet from which the hand has been abruptly withdrawn. I back out of the bathroom. I don't want to be in that room for another second.

The next thing I know I'm outside, walking fast back to my car. I don't really start shaking until I'm back on the causeway driving into the pulse of the city. Death is like some kind of hunter, chasing me down: California, Jacksonville and now Miami. It wants to run me right off the continent. It's all I can do not to drive off the edge of the world, to turn off Dixie Highway onto the street where I live, to pull into the gravel driveway and turn off the car.

Roy goes to a payphone and makes an anonymous call to the police. Then he holds me all night while I whimper. The next day I look in the papers. There is nothing about a dead body at the Fontainebleau. The blond-haired lady on Channel Ten doesn't mention him either.

Instead of taking my final exams, I go to the movies every day. I can't stay in Miami any longer. We buy a few doses of methadone from some junkies at the clinic and pack up our things. We drive back to Jacksonville, and I drop Roy and Stinky off at his parent's house and go to my Mom's apartment.

Then I call Charlie.

Crimson and Clover

I am sixteen years old. I am walking home from high school along Park Street. I hold my books against my chest; my long hair hangs down my back. Park Street is a busy street. The houses are old, two story--once rather grand, but some sections are falling into shabbiness. We still live in the house on Oak Street.

I'm walking down the street and I hear a horn honk. I start to whirl around and give the driver the finger. But when I look up, I see a familiar face. It is the face of the boy who lives in the big pointy-roofed house across the street. He is driving a furniture truck bearing his father's name. He smiles and waves at me. We don't really know each other except by sight. His name is Charlie. He is a couple of years older than I am. There is something sly and delicious in his heavy-lidded eyes. I smile back at him.

I know something has happened but I don't know what.

When we finally do meet, I have already shot heroin twice. We meet at a friend of mine's house--a boy who always rides to school with me in my Mazda. Charlie says to me, "Hello, pretty lady." And I am hooked.

I'm at my friend's house to cop some dope, and Charlie says in a surprised voice, "You get high?"

I shrug like, sure, of course, I do. He smiles and says, "I'm gonna marry you."

We get married one month after I graduate from high school. I walk down the aisle of the Episcopal church where my mother is the choir director in a beautiful white gown, scalloped neckline, tiers of lace down the skirt. My hair is long and gleaming. The wedding is forty minutes late in starting because Charlie was out trying to score heroin. It is obvious by the look of stupefaction on his face that he found some. I glance sidelong at him. He's not good looking when he is high. The people who are watching this seem as if they are unwilling participants in some sort of sacrifice. My mother has the look of someone going into a battle she knows she won't survive.

After the wedding, Charlie gets me off in the bathroom.

The reception is stupid and boring. We don't even have champagne. But we don't care because we don't drink anyway.

"You should look happy because you just got married, not because you're high," one of Charlie's friends says to me. This friend is the brother of Big Steve.

We drive to the beach and get a room at a high-rise hotel. The rain has already started and the wind is whipping crazy water snakes as we get out of the car. I'm wearing jeans as we go inside with our suitcases and check in.

Inside the hotel room, we look at each other and wonder what to do with ourselves, with each other. Charlie sits in the chair and stares out through the dark frothing water.

"I'm going to take a shower," he says and goes into the bathroom. I stare at the telephone and wonder who I should call.

I open my suitcase and take out my wedding dress which is crammed inside. I put the wedding dress on and go out onto the balcony. By now the wind is furious about something. The rain slants sideways and bursts against my skin, saturating the white dress. I hold onto the rail which is wobbling in the gusts. The door behind me whines in the wind. My hair flows sideways in a dark brown stream.

I sink down, holding onto the bars of the railing. A sentence is forming in my head the way words form in those old toy eight balls. You would ask the eight ball a question, shake it up and then turn it over to see the word that would emerge from the black liquid. And now the sentence that is taking shape in murk of my mind is this: I hate my life. I hate my fucking life.

Charlie opens the door.

"Jesus," he says and pushes against the wind. He takes my arm and pulls me inside. He has a towel wrapped around his waist.

“What the hell are you doing? Are you crazy?” he asks.

I just stare at him and then I go crawl under the covers of the bed.

“What’s wrong?” he asks.

I pull the covers over my head. He puts on a T-shirt and some boxer shorts and gets in the bed with me. I want to know why it’s all so wrong. I lean into him and taste his cotton T-shirt as I sob and the tears soak him.

And this was before I even had a habit. I should have paid attention to that girl on the balcony, but I guess she had to go through whatever was coming. Somehow, even then I knew it was going to get ugly.

Forget About Everything

Back in my mother's apartment in Jacksonville once again, I tried closing the books on Miami. It was summer, so I had the place to myself again. I decided I had to kick. No hospital this time. Charlie told me I could kick if I really wanted to. After all, he had gotten clean in prison and no longer had a habit. He looked good, a hell of a lot better than I did with my cross-stitch arms and my jeans hanging on my hip bones like old clothes on a coat hanger. I didn't want to go to the methadone clinic in Jacksonville, too many old cronies who could be bearing grudges. Charlie was living with his Momma. His father had died while he was in prison and his mother had gotten the big old brick house.

He came across the river every morning and fed me Jack Daniels and Valiums to help me kick. But I took too many Valiums; I forgot things. I forgot how many I had already taken. I kept swallowing little blue pills. I couldn't eat any food. I cried all the time.

"I'm gonna kill myself," I told Charlie. "Just like Angie."

"No, you aren't," he said. He hid the Valiums after giving me my morning dose. He tucked me under an afghan on the couch.

"Put on the album," I told him.

"Which one?" he asked. There were three that I listened to over and over--Billie Holiday, Barbra Streisand and Pink Floyd.

"Floyd," I insisted.

Then the familiar guitar whines would remind me of the first time I'd ever been high and a great cavern would open inside me, a cavern filled with yearning. What did I want so badly? I couldn't figure it out.

When I was clean, it was as if I had no filters, memories from my childhood wouldn't let me go—not just bad memories either. I might pick up a pecan and instantly fall down a well of memory like Alice tumbling through the rabbit hole and I would be eight years old again gathering pecans in the backyard with my mother. The present was just as weird, reality so raw I felt like a burn victim. The only thing that had ever stopped it, if only for a while, was dope, sweet sweet dope. I knew what I really wanted. I wanted to be a normal person, but I had no idea how to make that happen.

About the fourth day of my ordeal, Charlie figured he should take me out. So I spritzed my neck with Chanel No. 9, and we went to the Keg. He kept his arm draped over my shoulder as we were jostled around in the crowd.

"Hey, man, look who's out!"

Charlie shaking hands with some beer-swiller who I know hates him. Those people doing their eyeballs up and down and sideways. Charlie in that soft, smooth voice of his, saying: "Yeah, I got my lady back, too."

"Good to see you, Trish."

I nodded and looked away. Everyone in the place thought Charlie was a stinking junkie and I was a worthless slut. I didn't care what any of them thought. They were all too stupid and their lives were insipid, and I decided I'd rather be dead than be any of them.

"Let's get out of here, Charlie," I said.

We got back in the Cutlass, and we were heading home but when it came time to turn on to the Fuller Warren Bridge, Charlie kept going east.

“They’re a bunch of punks,” Charlie said.

I didn't say a word, just listened to the music on the radio--Gerry Rafferty's "Baker Street." He pulled off the exit to downtown.

"I wonder if any of those old cats still hang around down here?" he muttered. Everything was part of some accidental ballet. He drove along, just looking, you know, for no particular reason, leaving it all up to fate. Then he saw a dude he used to know. A smile broke like sunrise on his face.

"Hey, man, how you doin'?' he said out the car window as he pulled over.

The guy peered in at us and then his jaw dropped.

"My man Charlie!" he said. "You back out? Goddamn, man!"

I settled back in my seat. No one down here was going to judge me.

"Shit. You and your old lady down?"

"Naw, man. I'm clean," Charlie said. "And she's trying to get that way."

The guy looked over at me. I smiled weakly. His eyes were sympathetic.

"Shit, I got some good stuff," the guy said.

"Sho nuff?" Charlie asked in his imitation black cadence. The man nodded solemnly at Charlie.

"Tell you what, man," he said, "seeing as how you just got out of the joint, I'm gonna give you three bags out of my personal stash."

Charlie said, "Aw, man. You ain't gotta do that."

I was smiling all over inside.

Charlie pulled out twenty dollars and said, "Look here, gimme two and lemme buy two."

The guy gave us five bags for the twenty dollars — a remarkable act of generosity. We headed down the deserted downtown street toward the Hart Bridge over the dark water and toward home.

The next day Charlie and I started hitting up doctors for scripts of Dilaudids. There was a psychiatrist who would write scripts if you told him you were trying to kick heroin. We'd shoot as many of the Dilaudids as we could without dying and then sell the rest.

I was back on board the train.

One day there's a knock on the door of my mom's apartment. Charlie and I are good and fucked up, watching "General

Hospital." I go and open the door with Charlie right behind me. There's Roy.

"Aw, Roy. What are you doing here?" I ask him.

Roy snatches my wrist and looks at the new track marks.

"Look at this," he says, suddenly all concerned about my dope shooting habits.

"Hey, man, you need to leave," Charlie says.

Then Roy steps in the hallway and his fist slams into Charlie's gut. Charlie doubles over and groans. I start screaming. Roy hits Charlie again. The violence freaks me. I'm screaming and screaming, and the woman who lives next door sticks her head out.

She shakes her head and goes back in her apartment. Roy turns around and walks out the door like John Wayne. Charlie is slouched down against the wall.

Charlie still bent over, trying to catch his breath. Blood trickles from his mouth. I'm hoping that Roy didn't knock out one of his teeth, which aren't in good condition to begin with.

"Shit," he says. "We gotta get out of here. What if that bitch calls the cops? I'm gonna kill that motherfucker if I ever see him again."

I load up some clothes while Charlie waits in the car. Here we go again, running scared, I'm thinking as I throw a few books on top of the clothes. I wish we could stop running, but we gave it a shot, and it didn't work. It just didn't work. I figure nothing is going to help until I wind up like Paolo, dead in some bathroom.

I drive us down to the beach where we rent a room for a week.

The Lunatic in My Head

I was seventeen. Charlie and I had only been going out together a few months. It was a hot afternoon, and we were driving across the long windy bridge to the Eastside of town where Charlie's friend Damon lived in a small cinderblock duplex with his girlfriend Theresa. Before I started hanging around Charlie, I had never been in this part of town in my life. The poverty was startling and strangely comforting at the same time. Not that it was comforting to see people so poor, but there was a certain freedom here, an easiness to everything. I was naïve, of course, and it was easy to romanticize their lives. But it was still the 70s, and no one seemed to give a shit that Charlie and I were white.

The living room was cool and dark with red curtains over the windows. We would wait there while Damon went off to cop. Damon's girlfriend, Theresa, and I would talk while they were gone. Theresa was slender and doe-eyed with high cheekbones. We talked about our men, what they did that was good, what they did that made us want to kill them. Charlie wasn't much of a lover, but I didn't tell her that. It wasn't that he wasn't good, it's just that he wasn't interested. One time he used sex as an excuse to ask me for some money. I wasn't addicted yet, so his attitude baffled and infuriated me—like I have to pay for sex from my husband?

The first time I knew Charlie had a habit, we were in my car and I was driving. He wanted me to borrow twenty dollars from my mom.

"Why do we have to get some dope?" I asked. "Can't we just go to a movie or something?"

"Shit, baby," he said in a strange and desperate voice. "Can't you see that I'm sick."

Then I looked at him. His eyes were watery. His hands trembled and his whole body seemed to cave in on itself. I was instantly terrified. How had I not noticed this? What did it mean? I took my watch to the pawn shop, and we got off. And then I knew he would have to get high every day, and I would too. And eventually I would know what that meant—to be sick.

We are at Theresa's apartment. Charlie is standing in the bathroom with a needle hanging out of the back of his arm. He pulls the barrel back and it fills with blood. Then he pushes it in and pulls it back out again. I look down at the sink, and it is crawling with cockroaches. Theresa says she can't afford bug spray. I ignore the roaches and do my shot. The heroin gathers at the back of my throat and pulls my entire being with it. I vomit effortlessly into the toilet. I want to wash out my mouth but there is a roach on the faucet handle. We go into the living room, we sit and the day slowly spins past us like a movie in a foreign language.

A few weeks later we are at the county courthouse. Theresa and Damon are getting married. Theresa looks lovely in a blue dress, and Damon is dressed in a snazzy suit. He has a lean hip look. Charlie and I are their witnesses. After the J.P. pronounces them man and wife, he waits for some kind of payment. When it doesn't seem to be forthcoming, he asks Damon, "Aren't you going to pay me something?"

"Sorry, man, I ain't even busted my digit yet," Damon says and we walk out laughing.

It didn't take me long to learn the language. "Busted my digit" meant cash my check, of course. "Fat" was a term of approbation. Like some woman was "fat to death" or "fat to dizzum." To be "straight" meant to have dope. To be "greasy" meant to be really slobbering high. "Get down" was synonymous with "get high." And "skol," which I have no idea how to spell, was a gin and grapefruit juice concoction that Damon and Charlie liked to drink when we didn't have money for dope. They'd laugh and talk about how some guy they ripped off would whine and cry "like a bitch."

Charlie never did any kind of serious crimes. Mostly he just conned other people out of their money, and so he developed an ugly reputation since the people he conned were people that he knew. I helped him do this a few times. What happened was that my jaw began to tighten up and my stomach twisted so that I had these constant shooting pains and I couldn't open my mouth more than about a half an inch. Charlie got busted for stealing some stereos and sent to a drug program, but then he split the program and violated his probation. Soon there was a warrant out for his arrest, so we were fugitives.

One day we were at Damon's mother's house, and I was sick of it, sick of all of the running and the bullshit. I told Charlie I was going over to my Mom's to get some clean clothes. There weren't any arrest warrants out for me so I was safe to go home. I went to her apartment over on the Southside and instead of just getting some clothes, I got in the tub and took a long hot bath. Finally, I figured I better go back and get Charlie. So I drove back over to the little wooden house where Damon's mama lived, only instead of finding Charlie, Damon's mom came out and started yelling at me, saying to get out of there, she didn't need any more white folks causing trouble. Then Damon said Charlie was sitting on his mama's porch when the police drove by. As soon as they saw a white boy in a black neighborhood, they stopped. That was the end of Charlie's run.

He never brings it up, you know—the fact that if I hadn't been fooling around, taking a bath and all, he wouldn't have gotten popped. We're older and more desperate now, and we're together again. That's all that matters.

Reunited

By the end of the week, Charlie and I don't have any money. He's still nursing a bruise from when Roy socked him. We scrounge up just enough to eat breakfast at the Beach Diner on Saturday morning, but that's it. Then we sit around in the little room watching the black and white TV, feeling claustrophobic but too lethargic too move. There aren't even any doctor offices open. Finally, Charlie and I get in the car and go over to his mom's. She isn't home, but Charlie manages to con five bucks out of his brother.

"Well, we can get some burgers," I suggest.

"Or some cough syrup," he says.

"That's fucking pathetic," I tell him, but I drive to the drugstore and go into the pharmacist and give her this Betty Davis routine about my husband being sick and the only kind of cough syrup that will help him sleep is Robitussin AC. She slant-eyes me, but goes in the back and comes out with a small bottle of codeine cough syrup and makes me sign a book for it.

Outside, Charlie and I each drink half the bottle and head back to the beach.

The next day, Sunday, is even worse. The old man who owns the house where we renting a room wants to know whether we are staying for another week, and if so, where's the rent money? He's standing in the doorway, bleary eyed and smelling of salami.

"Sure, we want the room for another week," Charlie says. "But I won't have any money until the bank opens tomorrow. Can you wait until then? I'm good for it, I promise. I would have gone on Friday, but I had a business appointment and it lasted a lot longer than it should. You know how construction guys are. Anyway, Trish and I are planning to get up at the crack of daylight tomorrow and . . ."

The old guy turns around and walks away. Charlie figured he could win any argument just by talking long enough, and sometimes it worked.

About two that afternoon, Charlie says he's going to get a pack of smokes. I'm deep into Naked Lunch so I just nod my head. He walks out of the door and I hear the Cutlass engine roar. At that moment the little voice in my head pipes up, saying, don't expect him back anytime soon. I jump up and go look out the window. The car is slinking down the road.

When I finish the book, it's already getting dark. I haven't eaten all day, and Charlie has the damn car. I go outside and sit on the porch where I can smell the ocean a few blocks away. I'm thinking about how I'll snatch the keys from his hand and get in the car, how I'll peel rubber down the road. I would go for a walk, but what if he comes back while I'm gone. I'm edgy as hell although my habit is minimal now. I've gone into stasis which is an ability you develop pretty quick if you live this life. There is a time for action and a time for sitting like a statue. What I think about while I'm waiting is the scar on Charlie's hand. We'd only been married a month and I said the whole thing was a lousy, stinking mistake.

I'm remembering the scene: me, standing in front of my Mom's apartment with the door open, and him, on the sidewalk asking what the hell was wrong. His face had gone frantic. I don't want this, I said over and over. Then he pulled out his buck knife from his pocket and opened it. I was just standing there with my hands on my hips, looking at him like he was Bugs Bunny. He held out his left hand to me and then with his right hand, he sliced into the fatty part of his palm. Blood spilled all over the concrete walkway and I screamed. He cut so deep that he severed a nerve and his little finger never worked quite right after that. How did we all get so crazy, I wonder.

Finally, the Cutlass pulls up in front of the house. I'm still in stasis so I don't jump up and start selling tickets. When Charlie gets out, I can see that he's got somebody with him--a big dark-haired guy with a mustache and a big grin. They come loping up the steps and Charlie smiles like he's just been gone a few minutes.

"Hey, baby," he says.

"Hey," I answer.

"You aren't mad at me, are you?" he asks. "Look here, I brought somebody to meet you. This is J.D. — my main man in the joint. J.D., this is my wife."

J.D. nods at me and says, "Nice to meet ya."

"Uh huh," I say, squinting my eyes up at this guy. He's got a friendly kind of bearish manner.

"A peizurty weizoman, bro'" J.D. says. Like I don't know carnie talk.

"Thanks," I tell him and stand up. His eyes open wide. "I hope y'all got something good to tell me or I'm getting right the fuck out of here. I haven't eaten all damn day and you go off for five hours for a pack of smokes. What did you have to do, grow the fucking tobacco?"

"Easy, baby," Charlie says. "J.D. here has got something to make you feel better."

“Yeah, well, don’t go around introducing me as your wife. We’re not married anymore.” Charlie bites the inside of his lip when I say this, and J.D. stares at a street light that is flickering on and off.

Charlie leads me and J.D. into the yellow-walled room. He gets a glass of water. J.D. drops a couple of Dilaudids on the dresser. These are the new kind of Dilaudids, the kind with a buffer in them. Still we can break them down with a little bit of effort.

"Yeah, Charlie, we got a sweet game going, me and the boys," J.D. is saying. I'm watching him closely. My instincts are telling me that he's all right, but he's a different sort of animal, that much I know. Charlie and I are basically city kids. J.D. has that rough country criminal air about him like I've seen in the movies. I'm watching the way he moves his big body around, studying the expression on his face that he keeps turning my way, trying to win my approval. I smile back at him with just my eyes, let him know that I think he's all right. And Charlie starts crushing up the Dilaudids.

"How does the game work?" Charlie asks.

"Well, you got to have three or four guys," J.D. says.

"Guys, huh?" I ask.

"Yeah," J.D. says. "You got two of them driving point cars to keep a lookout for the rollers, and one drives the crash car. Then you got somebody else in the crash car who does the actual window smashing. Boom. Right through the front door of the drugstore. Silent alarm goes off but hell, you're clear across town by the time the police get there."

"What about the loudmouth alarm?" Charlie asks.

"Yeah, it goes off, too," J.D. says, "but that's why you got the point cars. The crash car doesn't even go up to the drugstore until the road is completely clear. And you got to be fast. One minute inside max."

Charlie gives me a needle with my Dilaudid in it. For a minute I forget all about J.D. as I do my shot. I'd been sitting there with my guts about to come out my asshole, but as soon as that warm orange liquid gets in me, I am perfectly fine all over inside and out. I clean out my needle and turn to J.D.

"Thanks for the D's," I say. I rub Charlie's shoulder, let him know that everything is O.K. I'm waiting for him to make the next move. We need a new game more than we need anything else right now.

"So how can I get in on this?" Charlie asks him.

J.D. shrugs. "I don't know, man. These guys are real hincty. And they're big-time, too. I mean, one of 'em is on the ten most wanted list."

Crickets and katydids commence with the nighttime concert outside the window. The ocean hums in the background.

"I'm hungry," I announce. The dope has brought back my appetite.

"Well, let me buy y'all a couple of burgers," J.D. says all hearty. "Hell, I owe old Charlie a few favors."

We head outside. All my shirts for the summer have 3/4-length sleeves to hide my track marks. But now I'm wearing a tank top underneath and in the dark I feel safe enough to bare my arms. The summer night is warm as liquor. J.D.'s footsteps tick tock on the sidewalk behind me.

Quicker Than They Thought

J.D. gives Charlie enough money for me to go to a doctor and complain about kidney pains. It's getting harder and harder to get a Dilaudid scrip out of a doctor. We're supposed to split the D's with J.D. when we get them. Apparently, the boys—whoever they are—haven't done a window smashing in a week or so. When we get the prescription, we go over to the drugstore by my mom's apartment to get it filled.

Then we go to my mom's place, where we're camping out ever since we snuck off from the beach house in the middle of the night.

Charlie and I get off in the bathroom and then go downstairs to settle into our high. We don't have much to say. We're both wondering what the hell we're doing. My mom will be back from North Carolina soon and then we can't stay here. And there are no more doctors. We'd had to go way the hell out to Orange Park to hit this one, and he said if I came back, he'd put me in the hospital for a kidney operation. Charlie's been bugging J.D. about getting in on the drugstore window-smashing action, but J.D. keeps saying he doesn't think the other guys'll go for it. But I've got a piece of information that's wandering around inside me, waiting for me to blurt it out. I chew on it a while and then I say to Charlie while I'm staring out the wall, "I saw where he got the D's."

"Who?"

"The pharmacist."

Charlie doesn't say anything for a minute. Then he whistles and asks, "Where?"

"Fourth row, second shelf," I answer.

We stare at each other, our thoughts like two computers transferring information.

"Should we tell J.D.?" I ask.

Charlie shakes his head. I smile.

"We'll do it ourselves," Charlie says. "That'll show 'em."

So first thing we do is go over to the other side of town and sell two of the Dilaudids from our prescription. Then we buy a sledge hammer, some gloves and a ski mask.

We watch Johnny Carson that night. But we're so nervous that every joke the man cracks just hurts. Charlie gets up every few minutes and paces around the living room. The Tonight Show ends, and we turn off the TV.

"How long should we wait?" Charlie asks.

"We should get it over with," I answer.

He nods.

Inside I am a trembling fool, my bowels doing flips. Charlie looks calm enough but he keeps biting the inside of his mouth. I can tell by the way he sucks his cheek in on one side.

We get in the Cutlass and Charlie lights a cigarette.

"All right," he says. "You're gonna pull up alongside of the store, right? Let me out. Then go to the far side by the supermarket and wait for me."

"Why don't I just wait by the store?" I ask him.

"No." He is adamant. "I don't want you taking that risk. If I get caught, baby, I'm gonna need someone to bail me out. You hear me? If something gets weird, you haul ass."

"All right. All right," I tell him. I do and don't like this concern of his. I want to be with him. I want to be as tough as he is and to get as close to danger as he does. But the other truth, the central truth, is that I don't want to go to prison. Prison is like death.

That night, as I drop Charlie off by the drugstore and drive through the black alleyway behind the supermarket over to the other side, I hear that old chilly voice in my head saying, just like death, prison is inevitable. I tell the voice to shut up.

When I get to the other side of the supermarket, I look carefully down the big highway and down the side road beside me. When an empty space opens up with no headlights from any direction, I flash my lights off and then on. A few moments later, I hear the crash of glass and the ringing of a loudmouth alarm. I breathe in deep. The world has not collapsed below the tires of my car. No blue lights surround me. Nothing has happened except for that annoying buzzing. I start counting. It takes approximately one minute and twenty seconds—the longest part is the run past the supermarket. And then Charlie is in the car, saying, "Drive, baby, drive. Drive carefully. Easy does it."

At first I push too hard on the accelerator because I am so frightened. The road wavers below us. My heart has wedged itself up between my ribs. Then I ease up on the gas. I tell myself that I am just an ordinary person out driving home. The light is red.

"Don't run it," Charlie says.

The light turns green, and a few minutes later I pull into the parking lot of my mother's apartment building. We get out calmly and go inside. We stand there for about ten minutes or maybe it's ten hours. Time is doing strange things. It is warping and expanding and contracting like a woman giving birth. And we are the strange aliens who are emerging. We're both standing while this is happening, me with my arms crossed, leaning against the dining table and Charlie with his hands in his pockets staring at the floor. Both our hearts hammering. Then slowly my hand reaches over to his.

"We did it," he says.

Taking Care of Business

The next day Charlie and I went over to the apartment where J.D. lived with his girlfriend of the moment, a dark-haired dancer with a vicious temper. She had started kicking at the windows of J.D.'s car with these big sparkly-heeled shoes a few nights ago, screaming at the top of her lungs about something J.D. did or didn't do, and Charlie and I had disappeared quick before someone called the cops.

She was still sleeping when we got to the apartment. We sat down on the couch tight up next to each other, and J.D. sat across from us in a lazyboy.

"All right," J.D. said, his eyes sliding from Charlie to me and back to Charlie. "What is it?"

"What's what?" I asked.

"If I had a feather up my ass I might be as tickled as you two seem to be," J.D. said and narrowed his eyes at us.

Charlie reached into his pocket and pulled out the bottle of D's. It was a pharmacy bottle, not a prescription bottle. Charlie rattled them around. That damn bottle was nearly full. He set them down on the coffee table next to a metal ashtray full of red lipsticked Newport butts and looked up at J.D.

J.D. sat up straight and stared at the bottle.

"Where'd you get those?" J.D. asked.

"Me and her did a drugstore last night," Charlie said.

"You and her?" J.D. asks and points at me.

I smirk at J.D. He thinks women can't do shit except dance in titty bars. J.D. laughs.

Then he says, "Y'all didn't really need to go and do that by yourselves. Turns out two of our esteemed colleagues have had to leave the state. So all that's left is me and McGuire. We was fixing to invite you into the group anyway."

I have a feeling that he means Charlie and not me. Well, we're a team now, and they've got me whether they want me or not.

He picks up the phone. He dials a number and says, "Yeah, McGuire. It's me. I got somebody I want you to meet." Then he looks over at me. "Make that two somebodies."

Man of Means

McGuire lives in a trailer. In the front of the trailer is a brand new silver Thunderbird. The drugstore business must be good—especially if you don't shoot all your profits. Charlie admires the car as we head up to the door. McGuire shakes Charlie's hand and nods at me. Two lanky preteen kids stand behind him.

"These are my boys," he says. "Go on now, y'all go play or something."

The boys squirm past him.

"Their momma's in prison," McGuire says. "Y'all come on in."

The trailer is neat, and the furniture looks new. We sit down on a couch with a plastic cover.

"Nice place," Charlie says.

McGuire nods. He has gray eyes and copper colored hair. As I sit there on the couch, I try to figure out what it is about him that intrigues me. His voice is friendly, and there's a glint in his eyes. He's older than us by maybe ten years. He and Charlie talk for a few minutes about prison, establish who was where when like old soldiers remembering their battalions. McGuire has a faded tattoo of a rose on his arm, his face is gaunt as if he's missing some teeth.

A woman in her 30s comes in, wiping her hands on a dishtowel. McGuire introduces her. Her name is Anita; she's got frosted hair and wears little silver slippers on her tiny feet. I remember hearing J.D. say that Anita is McGuire's wife's sister and she has a serious reputation as being into big-time stuff, though he never elaborated. Her hand is draped on McGuire's shoulder as she asks us if we're staying for dinner, and I have the feeling that she's taken her sister's place in more ways than one.

"Naw, I don't think so," J.D. tells her. "Thank you much."

And Charlie says to her in his soft sweet voice, "That's nice of you to offer. Maybe some other time."

She smiles at Charlie. All women like Charlie. It's those deep eyes and good manners.

She leaves and McGuire looks at us.

"Y'all stay for a bit and watch the news," McGuire says, flicking on the big console television. We settle back in the sofa. I look at J.D.'s big neck and the gold chain that he wears. Charlie's face is relaxed, impassive.

On the television Jimmy Carter is getting raked for something having to do with his pal, Bert.

"I wish like hell they'd leave old Jimmy alone," McGuire says. I know that no one in this room has ever voted, but as southerners we all like Jimmy Carter, especially now when he's just looking at the reporters with this blank smile, as if he's asking them, don't they have something better to do with their time. He ignores their questions about Bert and starts talking about the oil crisis.

"He's a good old boy," J.D. says.

"I like Rosalyn," I tell them.

"She's a fine lady, a fine lady," McGuire says. "She's got class."

Then McGuire looks over at me, and I can't read the look. I glance over at Charlie who doesn't say anything, just quietly smokes his cigarette. After the news, McGuire flicks the television off, and Anita comes back in.

"I made enough spaghetti for everyone," she says. "Come in and fix yourself a plate."

So we go into the kitchen even though we had declined her earlier invitation. I got the feeling she didn't take no for an answer — ever. McGuire's two boys come in and eat in the kitchen while we take our plates back to the living room. We eat hungrily. And when we're done, McGuire wipes his mouth with a paper towel and finally talks about the reason we're here.

"Well, they's a full pharmacy over there out Beach Boulevard. It's the onliest place I know exactly where the D's are, right off hand. Y'all want to hit it tonight?"

"Definitely," Charlie says. "You just tell me where they are."

As we walk out the door, McGuire tells us to drive safely. He gives my shoulder a squeeze, and I realize that McGuire is some sort of father figure. We head back across town, flying along the swooping interstate.

The first drugstore we hit as a team is over near my mother's apartment. I drive one point car, sitting at an intersection with my citizen's band radio. McGuire drives another and waits at the next intersection. In between us is the drugstore. The shopping center is on a major thoroughfare and we have to wait for what seems like forever before there is no traffic even at 4 in the morning. My stomach squeezes in on itself and I can't stop yawning because I am starting to need a fix. Finally, I look down and the road stretches out emptily.

"Clean and Green," I say into the handheld mic of my CB radio.

Then I hear McGuire's voice: "Clean and green this way."

"All right, we're going in," J.D. says. The crash car race up to the drugstore. I'm not sure why we call it a crash car, and I'd look stupid if I asked. I know that one reason I'm accepted is that I don't ask a lot of questions. A few seconds later, the sound of glass shattering echoes in the empty night. I imagine Charlie running down the dimly lit aisles of the drugstore past toothpaste and diapers and then up over the counter to the drugs.

Less than a minute later, J.D. says "He's out. Go. Go. Go."

As we're driving to my mom's apartment, I hear McGuire asking on the C.B. how it looks.

"We got the D's," J.D. says. "I repeat, we got the D's."

This is more like it, I keep thinking. Maybe those begging days are finally over.

My mom's apartment is closest so that's where we go. We file into the apartment cool and quiet. Charlie has a wild exuberant look on his face.

"Damn, look at all these books," McGuire says. "You read all these books?"

"No," I tell him. "Not all of them. I don't play the fucking piano either."

J.D. goes over to the Steinway and plays a note, but Charlie gives him a dirty look. I know Charlie's scared, and a little sick. McGuire and J.D. aren't sick. They don't have habits. I wish we didn't either, but then I wouldn't be here, doing this, if we didn't.

"Come on, J.D.," McGuire says. "We got work to do."

We go through the laundry basket full of bottles of a variety of drugs. We scrape off the numbers for some reason. McGuire and J.D. insist that it's important though it seems to me that if you get busted with the drugs, you're going down no matter what. But they say it's a matter of going down for possession versus going down for possession and burglary.

"Hey, what's this?" J.D. asks. He holds up a big bottle of green liquid.

"It's cough syrup," Charlie says.

"What wrong? You got a cold?" J.D. asks with a laugh.

"Look at the label," Charlie says.

I look over J.D.'s shoulder and see the big Roman numeral two on the label. It's a class 2 narcotic.

"It's got Dilaudid in it," McGuire says, taking the bottle from J.D. "Well, you cain't sell this."

"I know," Charlie says. So McGuire unscrews the cap and hands it to me.

"Ladies first," McGuire says. I take a swig of the syrup and pass it to Charlie, who takes a swig and passes it on.

Thirty minutes later, we're all sitting on the rug, bent over, heads drooping toward the floor, swaying in a Dilaudid delirium. We're beyond the usual comfortable feeling of being high. Reality has become distorted, slowed down, turned inside out. I'm pretty sure that Angie is sitting on the couch behind me. But when I look for her, she isn't there.

I turn to Charlie and say, "Did you see Angie?"

"No," he says, "was she here?"

I nod and scratch my nose. My whole face itches. Then I remember that Angie is dead.

"She loved you, Charlie," I tell him.

"Good old Angie," he says. I wake up enough to take the cigarette from between his fingers and drop it in a Pepsi can so he won't burn us all to death.

No one else says anything until we finally start to ease ourselves back into the world. Morning comes. J.D. and McGuire leave, and Charlie and I curl up together. Finally, things will be easy for a while.

Pouring Rain

Charlie and I rented an apartment in some shitty complex. The place had hardly any windows and a hideous green velveteen sofa. We ate off Currier and Ives plates that we bought at the flea market. We watched General Hospital every day, ate cream of chicken soup and Kraft macaroni and cheese. We drank Pepsi-Cola every morning for breakfast.

And we shot Dilaudids fresh from the pharmacy on a regular basis.

What a pain in the ass those things were to cook up. We had to crush them (we'd put them in a piece of folded paper and use a glass to smash them down) and then mix the powder with boiling water in the barrel of the needle. Then shake and shake to try to get it to break down. But at least we always knew what we were getting—good narcotic every time. In the old days, when I first started shooting drugs, Dilaudids were white and did not all have that buffer in them. We called them "shake-em-ups."

Sometimes when we ran out of Dilaudids and hadn't hit another drugstore yet, we would shoot the leftover trash drugs that we'd gotten from the pharmacy. Those were the worst times in my life. Probably worse than kicking. Certainly worse than prison. Junkies lead a roller-coaster life. One day we've got a bottle full of number four Dilaudids, we're eating steaks at good restaurants and staying in decent motels or in our own apartment. A week later, we're out of town in a room that doesn't have carpeting on the floor and the bed sags to the ground and it smells moldy, and the grime and grunginess are unspeakable: roaches roaming the bathroom, dirt on the linoleum floor and the roar of semi-trucks on the road outside. And we're hoping when we get back in town and we stop by someone's house that they'll offer us something to eat.

We've been out of Dilaudids for about 36 hours. Charlie and McGuire and J.D. are going to hit a drugstore that night. The way the drugstore is situated they only need one point car, so I'm not going along. Staying home is worse, waiting, not knowing what's going on. I don't look forward to it. Outside a gray wall of rain surrounds us, and the air smells soggy. I am sitting by the open door just staring out at the rain when Charlie comes up and shuts the door.

I stand up and open it again. The apartment makes me claustrophobic. I hate the way it stinks of cigarette smoke. Charlie closes the door again.

"Fucker," I say. I get up and walk outside.

When it gets late, I go back inside. Charlie is sitting on the couch, smoking a cigarette and watching television. His cigarette smoke has permeated every square inch of this apartment. I decide I'll go down to the Minit Market for something to drink. I start to tell him this, but then when I look over at him, instead of saying Charlie, I say, "Roy." The word is half way out of my mouth when I realize my mistake. Charlie's eyes turn into two blue marbles.

"What did you call me?"

I'm trying to think of something I could have been trying to say that might start with the same sound. I'm searching desperately for the right lie to save me, but nothing comes.

"Damn it. I am not Roy." Charlie stands up.

"Sorry," I say.

"Sorry?"

I go into the bedroom. I just want to get away from him. But he follows me. Charlie has never hit me, never even threatened me. But he comes into the room and with the back of his hand, he smacks me across the forehead. I'm looking at the two of us in the mirror—his tensed-up back and my shocked face. It didn't even hurt which was strange in itself, and then he does it again.

I turn around and go to the dresser drawer. Inside is the chrome .38 special he traded some speed for. I pick up the gun and wheel around, pointing it at him.

We stare at each other for a long, long moment.

"If you're gonna pull a gun on me, baby, you better be prepared to use it," he says.

I don't know what to say so I don't say anything. I'm wondering if I can shoot him. It's a bad spot to be in. He's hit me. And I feel that I need to kill him for that. But if I kill him then he will not be able to hit the drugstore tonight. And I won't have any Dilaudids. Just then there's a knock on the door.

"That's J.D. and McGuire," Charlie says. "I'm going to go."

He walks into the living room and lets them in. J.D. is boisterous, loud.

"Hey, where's the little lady?" he calls out.

"She's in the bedroom," Charlie says. "I'll be right back."

Charlie comes back in the bedroom.

"Are you gonna be here when I get back?" he whispers to me.

I don't say a word. I can't. I know that he wonders if I'm pissed off enough to call the cops and get him busted since it is obvious by now that I'm not going to shoot him. I silently put the gun back in the drawer.

"All right. We're going," he says. Then he leaves.

A couple of hours later, they all tromp into the apartment.

Charlie has that wild look in his eyes that he always gets after he's been inside a drugstore in the middle of the night. He smiles at me, and kisses me on the cheek.

"Come on, baby," he says. "Let me fix up your shot."

I still don't say anything.

J.D. asks why I'm not speaking, and Charlie says, "She's mad at me. I was an asshole."

So he fixes up my shot, and I let him get me off. Then he does his own shot. And afterwards we give each other the traditional after-shot kiss. In the kiss everything is forgiven. McGuire and J.D. leave. We go to bed, our minds in a murky river where occasionally we see each other but for the most part we are just suspended in the deep murk, below pain, below anger, below everything that is terrible or simply unpleasant.

So Easy

During the day, Charlie and I bought things. Mostly we bought things from drugstores. Actually, I bought while Charlie scoped. Can you tell me which is the better contact lens solution, sir? Excuse me, ma'am, but I need some cough syrup for my little boy, which kind would you recommend. I had cabinets full of cold remedies, vitamins, antacids and laxatives. As soon as I got a look from Charlie, I knew the asking was over and we'd head back out. It was good to buy something. We never wanted to create suspicion. Charlie's azure eyes would almost always find the Dilaudids back on the shelves behind the pharmacist's counter.

We used to drive around town for hours. We had a white Monte Carlo that we rented by the month. It had a red interior. The song that was on the radio that summer was Gerry Rafferty's "Baker Street."

The radio was like a soundtrack to our lives—we were totally unhip to the alternative music scene, never went to concerts or bought records. I can still see Charlie, cigarette in his mouth, gazing off into the distant, while I drove us along some highway.

One time we went in a drugstore to scope it out. I had to pee and I asked the pharmacist where the bathroom was. It was an old drugstore and he pointed back behind the counter. I walked down a small aisle. On my way out of the bathroom, I noticed a small amber bottle with an orange seal around the top on the shelf as I was passing. I slipped the bottle into my pocket. Charlie and I went outside.

"Did you see the D's?" I asked.

"Hell, no," he said, pissed.

We got in the car.

I turned to him with a smile I couldn't repress and pulled out the bottle. Charlie's mouth dropped open. He took the bottle from me and stared at it. Then he leaned over and kissed me hard on the mouth. He bragged about that coup for a long time to all his friends. He always told J.D. and McGuire that I wasn't just his old lady, I was his partner.

For my twenty-second birthday, Charlie bought me a rabbit fur coat. We went to an Italian restaurant and had lasagna. We took pictures of each other. In the pictures I am never smiling. My skin is so white I look like a vampire. The flash makes my eyes red.

Sometimes we are up until dawn going after a drugstore. We don't even start until two or three in the morning. So it is just cracking light at the edge of the sky, and the roads are empty when we pull into the parking lot behind the apartments where we live. I park the car. We're quiet now, moving quickly. Charlie has already stashed the sledge hammer in the trunk along with laundry basket and his ski mask and gloves. He'll have a paper bag tucked under his arm filled with the drugs that we didn't throw away. The names of all the drugs begin with the letter D. We've already gotten off and split the drugs with J.D. and McGuire. Once in a while, Charlie has the foresight to slip something into his pocket while he is still in the drugstore so that we don't have to share it with the others. We'll go upstairs to our apartment at the end of the hall. Inside everything smells of cigarette smoke. Charlie will hide the drugs in an air conditioning vent. We'll sleep all day.

One time I broke up with Charlie and moved in with my mom. I tried to kick by drinking Jack Daniels and listening to my Billie Holiday record over and over. Good morning, Heartache, what's new? A couple of days later I went back to Charlie.

When I look back on those days, I feel like I'm watching a scary movie—the kind where you're always yelling at the girl not to go into the house or not to open that closet door. I want to scream at myself and say, "Don't do it. Don't go back. Stop now." But just like the girl in the movie, I always go into the house where the maniac is waiting, and I am both the maniac and the girl.

Wishing the Trip was Through

It was night. J.D. had gotten busted for possession of pot and was in the county jail. McGuire had broken his leg while jumping off a drugstore roof.

"Guess it's just you and me again, baby," Charlie said. We were cruising along I-10. I sniffled. I had refused to drive.

We had been driving all day though we only went ninety-four miles from point A to point B. Charlie was cool and distant, as far from me as the waxy water is from the high crest of the Buckman Bridge. In spite of our good intentions, we'd gotten on the methadone program, not to kick, just to hold us over in between drugstores. Now we were cross-addicted to Dilaudids and methadone, and our habits were monstrous. And for some reason, every time I closed my eyes, I kept seeing corpses. Sometimes they belonged to people I knew, sometimes they didn't. If the radio wasn't on, I'd hear Angie laughing or Big Steve crooning that country song.

"It's just us again," Charlie said, pushing in the lighter.

I didn't answer. I was sitting in the front seat with a package of van-o-lunch cookies that I was having for dinner. The sun had collapsed into a bed of red clouds in the distance.

"It's just us again," he repeated a few miles later.

As we traveled along I-10, I thought of how Big Steve and Timothy and Cynthia and I had taken this road all the way to California and how only three of us ever came back. And I thought again of Angie. What would she think of all this, I wondered. Would she tell me what I was telling myself, *that it wasn't fun anymore*?

Charlie and I were in a green Cutlass that I'd bought from some drug dealers who owned a car lot. What a find these guys had been—buying all our speed and Demerol and stuff we didn't want, and providing cars to use. That morning, the dude running their operation asked, "Where's your partners, man?"

"They'll be there," Charlie lied.

"Well, I gotta know how far you gonna take this car," he said.

"Just outside Lake City," Charlie said. "We'll have it back in the morning. With plenty of D's."

"How about black beauties?" the guy wanted to know. "You gonna have any? I got a lot of customers for those amphetamines you brought in last time."

"Yeah, yeah. This place is loaded," Charlie said. "Fat and lonely. My kind of date."

They handed over the keys to a gray Pontiac, and we were on our way.

"Why are you so sulky, baby?" Charlie had asked.

"Because I feel like it," I answered.

Around twilight, we pulled off the interstate, and suddenly Charlie slowed way down.

"What are you doing?" I asked.

"You didn't see that?" he asked.

"What?" I looked around, thinking cops must be close by, but all I saw was a car on the side of the road, one of those big road hogs that old people drive. The emergency flashers beat out a cry for help. Charlie had pulled over and started backing up.

"What the hell?" I asked.

"I'm gonna help her," he said.

I stared at Charlie. His lips were pursed, the skin tight on his bones. Then I turned and saw an older woman looking helplessly down at the rear tire on her old heavy car. I wanted to laugh, but then thought better of it. This was the little thing, the shred of the original Charlie, in operation. He'd kept this one piece of goodness. I wondered if I had any left in me.

We got a motel room and waited. Time fell at our feet, one minute at time. About 3:30 in the morning, we stood up and went outside. There were no stars in the sky, just a thick blanket of cloud. For some reason I thought of a stomach lining. We were in the belly of some enormous creature and didn't even know it.

Charlie sat in the passenger seat, smoking quietly as I pulled off the interstate and drove past the shopping center, which was sprinkled with the cool, plastic light of streetlamps.

This is the time I like the best. No one else is out, the whole earth as quiet as outer space.

"Why do you suppose there's a camper in the parking lot?" Charlie asks.

"Someone left it there?"

"I don't know. Maybe."

He doesn't say anything. I drive down the road, and then turn around.

"Well, what do you think?" I ask him. He takes a drag from his cigarette, looks down at his hands and then back out the window.

"Fuck it," he says. "We gotta do it."

"O.K." I'm glad we're going for it. I want to get high, want to feel right again, want to escape the chasm growing inside me. A part of me knows it's hopeless. A part of me knows this isn't working anymore.

"Don't wait out front for me," Charlie says as we pull into the lot. "Go to the street, and flash your lights if no one is coming. When I'm out, I'll come to you. Just like the first time, baby. Just like the first time."

I do as he says and then look back.

Black silhouettes move across the parking lot. Who are they? What are they doing there suddenly like apparitions? Then I see the shape of the long rifles they're carrying, see them slide between my car and Charlie, see my hand pull the gear shift down to D. Bullets plunk into the side of the car as I haul ass through the dark night, along the invisible road as the rain falls and mixes with oil on the surface of the tar.

From out of nowhere police cars scream. My blood sears my veins in terror.

"Were you fuckers cloaked or what?" I scream, looking in my rearview mirror. My car hydroplanes on the slick wet road. I can feel my heartbeat in my hands. I can't see a fucking thing. Don't turn on your headlights, fool, I tell myself. I keep the headlights off, but it doesn't help. They are right on me like hornets. I'm gonna die. I am going to die tonight. The sound of sirens wraps around my neck. I feel like an animal, a wild animal pursued by braying dogs.

That Cutlass goes a hundred miles an hour until it starts spinning pirouettes, and the rain and the streetlights fly around me in a brilliant blur. Everything happens slowly then. The car whirling around and around and around and then sliding off the road and landing with a thud in the ditch, the nose of the car about five inches from the trunk of a tree. Fortunately, I was wearing my seatbelt.

Thirty Days in the Hole

I lay in the middle of the road, my hands linked together in cold metal handcuffs behind my back, watching the rain splatter on the road, watching the black shoes of the police as they walked around in the swirling blue and red light. How had they known? I kept wondering. And this song by the Grateful Dead revolved around my brainpan, "Set up like a bowling pin. Knocked down gets to wearing thin."

It wasn't until hours later when I was in the jail, freezing under a thin blanket in a cell by myself, that a scene popped up into my head: Charlie telling the drug dealing car dealer, "Just outside Lake City." Then that voice piped up and said, "You chumps. Told the police where you were going."

I thought about what I should have done—should have just slipped the car into park and slid out the passenger door, headed for the woods and to the interstate on foot. I could have gotten away. Maybe. I replayed those last few hours over and over. Why didn't we know that camper was a bad sign? Why didn't we even think cops would be hiding inside? But I knew this, and I guess Charlie did, too: If not tonight, then the next one or the next one.

I settled down and got ready to be real sick. Waiting for it to hit was like standing on the beach, waiting for a hurricane. Everything was just a sign of what was coming. In a way, I hoped the pain would be really bad, bad enough to knock me unconscious, bad enough that I wouldn't think about how lonely I was. I wondered about Charlie. How was he doing? I lay in the big cell all by myself. The yellow walls smothered me.

The next morning it started. The diarrhea, back ache, runny nose, puking. There wasn't anything separating me from myself anymore. I had to be inside me. I kept having this fantasy that someone was going to walk inside the cell and give me a shot. I hit the walls with my fist to get the fantasy out of my head.

A chubby little Lake City Deputy came to the window and asked if I was "gonna have fits."

I told her no, and she turned away as if she was slightly disappointed.

They gave me food, but I couldn't touch it. Water leaked out of my nose, my eyes, my ass. A few days later, I couldn't even tell you what year it was.

After a week my mom got me a good lawyer, who arranged for me to see a private doctor who gave me some big green pills to help me sleep. A girl in the cell next door thought I was some kind of Jesse James because I had led the police on a car chase and everyone was excited about that because I was a girl and all. She would pass Harlequin romances to me through the bars along the catwalk; there was a wall between us. I never could see her, but we talked a lot. I hated those romances but I read every one. And cried over them. The tears felt good.

I got out a few weeks later and headed to drug program number two in Gainesville. I should have just gone to prison then and gotten it over with. Charlie got another dime. Sayonara, baby.

Last Chance

Drug Program Number 2. Like the first drug program, this one had a thousand nit-picky little rules and they loved for you to occupy your time by cleaning. Instead of sweeping stairs, however, I raked dirt. Hours and hours of making little lines in the dirt. I stayed in a dorm with three girls, who were way younger than I was--they were like preschoolers, still playing with crayons. But they were nice enough and easy to get along with when they weren't giggling like the adolescents that they were. They kept me up all night, and sleep was precious hard to come by. I felt edgy and irritable, and they wanted to listen to disco. I couldn't figure out what they were doing in a drug program in the first place.

The main house was full of boys. I met two guys who had actually been dope shooters at some point in their lives. I became pals with them and a couple of the other guys, including a guy named Randall with alcohol problems and a riotous sense of humor. My first Saturday the whole house got into a water fight with buckets, water balloons, water guns. I tried to stay out of the way, but Randall came along and doused me with a pail of water. Then he poured flour on top of me. I would have killed him, but I was laughing too hard.

Presiding over it all from her perch on the porch was Barb, the assistant director of DP No. 2. Barb came from Miami, a former junkie of the high, high order of old dope fiends. I admired Barb. Hell, I idolized her. When her eyes turned into cold stones and she blasted, why don't you go fuck yourself, I could only think of Moses standing on the mountain raising hell with idolatrous Jews.

But Barb didn't tell me to go fuck myself. I was the first bona-fide junkie to come into the program in a while, and she treated me like I was her long lost cousin. She called me up to her office the first night I was there — still dope sick and skittish. She and three or four other residents were hanging out, calling in requests to the Sunday night oldies show.

"We requested a special song just for you," she said with a laugh. I sat down nervously and waited. The rest of them all joked around with her. Then the song came on: "I fought the law and the law won."

She burst out laughing. I said, "Yeah, that's a good one."

I felt like someone from another planet, and I explained to myself that this was how the natives had fun and they didn't mean any harm. But as soon as I could, I moseyed back downstairs to the dorm room and climbed up on to my bunk for a restless, evil night, while the dope need tortured me. All the while that song rocked back and forth in my head.

Barb would sometimes take a few of us to the coffee shop in town. It was a small wood paneled place with backgammon boards painted on the thickly varnished cedar-knee tables. The coffee came in dozens of varieties and they had this cannoli that you would trade a kidney for.

We'd order a pot of the day, and Barb would talk to us about any old shit--nothing really earth-shattering. She'd rag on other women, the way they were dressed or something, or she'd talk about how lame other drug programs were. While we were there, I'd see college women with their boyfriends, intently huddled over coffee, with their dark hair and that air of knowing so much more than the rest of the world. I wanted to be one of them. I had no idea how to do it, but it looked better than what I'd been doing.

One day the whole house took a field trip to play softball at a local park. I used my bum knee as an excuse not to play, and instead I walked around the field by myself. Pine trees dotted the rim of the field. I smelled the pine needles on the ground. A very soft rain began to fall even though the sun was shining. The rain felt like pastel colors in the warm air. I could hear the shouts of people playing softball and having fun. For the first time in what seemed like a thousand years, I felt naturally good. And I thought, maybe I can do this. Maybe I can live my life this way.

When we got back to the house, a new resident had been sent over from the courts.

"One of your homeys," Barb said to me. She was sitting on the porch with one of the counselors. I walked in the living room to get a peek at the new recruit. He turned around and gazed up at me with his pock-marked face and choirboy grin.

"Jasper Collins," I said.

Over the Line

One day in early June, the house took a trip to the lake. We girls wore our bikinis. I had a white one that helped me not look so pale. We ate hotdogs and watermelon. Barb sat next to me on the blanket, her legs brown, her knees wrinkly.

"Dope is not your problem, Trish," she said to me.

"It's not?" I asked.

"Nope," she said. Above us live-oak limbs, heavy with gray Spanish moss, shaded us like patient slaves.

"So what am I doing in my second drug program then?" I asked.

"Your problem is men," she said, leaning up on her elbow. She had brown eyes like my mom's and a sharp fox face.

"Do tell," I said.

"You see, everyone has a certain programming inside them, Trish. This programming tells them to mate. It's how the species is propagated," she said. I couldn't see where she was going with this. "But in your case, you've had to sabotage the programming."

"Why would I do that?" I asked.

"Look at your history," she said as if I was totally blind. "All your experience has shown you that to be involved with a man is dangerous, that men are treacherous, and so you use drugs to try to counteract the programming. But you're still drawn to men. The only problem is that you're scared to death. So you take dope, you dope."

"My brother isn't treacherous," I said.

"He left when you were six years old," Barb said. "To a six-year-old that's abandonment, honey. You better face it. Your problem is with men."

I thought she was crazy, but I wasn't going to tell her that. Instead I got up and said I was going in for a swim.

The lake water looked maple syrup but felt like silk. There's something about the way lake water tastes, like it's the mother's milk of the earth, that just intoxicates me. I sank under the water and let it run its fingers through my hair which was starting to grow long again. I came back up to the surface and saw Randall and the others holding onto some poles thrust out from the dock. I swam over. It felt great to move my body like that. Almost as good as a drug.

Two of the girls were hanging on the boards, flirting with Randall who was opposite them. I sidled up next to them. By now I got along with the girls, and Randall had been my laughmate from the beginning. The teenage boys were jumping off the end of the dock. I saw Jasper sitting on the dock, sulking. I'd been ignoring him since he got in the program, not because I didn't like him anymore. It's just that I was afraid of getting caught up in the old shit. When I thought of Jasper, I thought of shooting Dilaudids in his dad's church, I thought of the colored light coming through the stained glass windows as we sat in the pews nodding off, and I could hear that familiar call though it was fainter than it had been.

Randall's leg bumped against mine. Our eyes flicked toward each other and away. I felt his leg rub against my skin again. I felt drowsy with the sun on my head and the warm water lapping against my shoulders. After a few minutes the girls left, and Randall moved over so he was opposite me. Our legs intertwined softly. We didn't say anything. The sound of everyone else grew faint.

We hadn't planned it. If we had, it never would have worked. In a few minutes, Randall and I were both naked from the waist down and we were gently, oh so quietly, fornicating below the dark covering of the water. We were breaking a cardinal rule of the drug program, which said no sex, ever, between residents. And we were doing it right in front of everyone. His eyelids lowered. I bit my lip. He let out a soft moan. I exhaled. And then we opened our eyes and stared at each other. Words failed us.

Later I was back on the blanket on the green grass, and one of the girls asked me why my bathing suit bottom was on inside out.

"I must have put it on that way this morning," I said, nonchalantly and walked to the public restroom where I slipped on my jeans and decided I wouldn't go swimming anymore that day.

In the van on the way back, I sat next to Barb.

"Why did you say that about me and men?" I asked her. "I mean, how do you know that?"

"Because it was true for me, too. When I was twelve, my father started to put his hands where they didn't belong. You know what I mean?" Then she leaned over. "He stuck his fingers inside me. Inside me. I was only twelve years old."

I closed my eyes. I could hear Randall in the front seat, laughing with one of the other guys.

"And you know, the funny thing is that last year when he was dying, he called and asked me to come see him. I told him to fuck himself," she said.

I wanted to say something, but I didn't know what was appropriate.

When we got back to the center, I had a surprise waiting for me. My mother had brought the Cutlass. I was told that once I made Level 3, I'd be able to use it to drive the residents to doctor's appointments or for other errands. These fools thought it would be okay for me to have some responsibility. And I was an even bigger fool because I believed it, too.

Bring Me Dead Flowers

The next day Jasper finally cornered me.

"I got to talk to you after dinner," he said. "Privately."

We ate in shifts at a big dining table. We had hamburgers that night. I was starting to gain some weight.

"All right," I said.

"Where can we go?" he asked.

"Meet me by the girls' dorm at 9:30," I said. I would hear what he had to say.

At 9:30 after the card games were over and everyone was engaged in the final clean up, Jasper and I slipped behind the girls' dorm.

"What is it?" I asked.

"You gotta hold something for me," he said.

"What?" I asked.

"My works," he said.

"Hell, no," I said. "Why give them to me?"

"Cause I have to go to court tomorrow," he said.

"No way, Jasper. Get rid of them," I said.

Jasper got into my space and he was practically pleading with me. I could smell ketchup on his breath from the hamburgers. He was just a few inches taller than I was. I'd known him for so long, longer than anyone else it seemed.

"Please," he said. "Just for one day. Then you can give them back to me."

"You fucking asshole," I said.

He held out his hand with one red-capped needle in it, and I took it, felt the needle in my hand like a familiar weapon, and then stuck it into my underwear. I walked back into the yard without saying anything.

That night after sweeping off the porch, I went to the dorm with the other girls. I didn't know what to do with the works. I thought I might flush them the next day, but for the meantime,

I slipped them between the sheet and the mattress of my bed. I got into my PJs and lay down. The girls were giggling, but finally they fell asleep.

I lay awake for a while. I wasn't thinking about the works or Jasper. I was thinking about Randall and having sex that day in the lake. How good it felt and not just that we were getting away with something, but the actual sex. When was the last time I'd had sex without being high? I couldn't remember. Maybe Barb was right. Maybe I'd been sabotaging myself, trying to erase a need I didn't even know I had.

I had just drifted off when the counselors started banging on the doors.

"Guilt session."

Aw fuck, I thought, throwing the covers off me. It was just like New York. What kind of idiot rats on herself, I wondered. The other girls were all whining and complaining. Barb stuck her head in the door and told us all to shut up.

"Get in the living room and no one says anything," she said.

So we trundled on into the living room. Everyone was in there, tired and disgruntled, hair messed up. I caught Randall's eye, asking him with a look if this guilt session was because of us. He shrugged his shoulders slightly. I figured that meant he hadn't said anything. I sat down on the floor next to the worn out old couch and stared at nothing. The counselors paced around the room. I suddenly remembered Jasper's works, and I got a really sick feeling.

We sat there for a couple of hours. Every once in a while someone would get up and go into the counselor's office to snitch on themselves. Finally, about midnight, Barb comes in and stands over in a corner and looks straight at me.

"You got some guilt you want to cop, Miss Level Two Resident?" she asked, meaning I had come up in the program and so I had a responsibility to snitch on myself.

"Should I have?" I asked her.

"Seems somebody saw you and your homey slip behind the girls dorm tonight," she said. Her eyes were cold, not angry, just cold.

I looked over at Jasper, and he just hung his head.

"You know that sex between residents is violating a cardinal rule," she said. There were only three cardinal rules, the other two were possession of drugs or guns.

I put my head in my hands. Just like high school, I was thinking. Just like high school only now the stakes are so much higher.

"It isn't what you're thinking," I said. But then some kid who sleeps in Randall's room piped up.

"What a slut," he said. "Randall told me he did it with her in the lake."

I stared at Randall. He closed his eyes and grimaced.

Barb laughed a mirthless laugh.

"Whoa, payday," she said. Then she got serious and said, "You better hit the road, girl."

It took a moment to register what she'd said. No one made a sound.

"Pack your shit and get out," she said.

I slowly stood up. I wondered if she was also going to kick out Randall. Probably not. I don't know why I knew she wouldn't, but I knew it. So I walked out of the room. A few boys snickered when I walked out. I could hear them even as I went out the back door. I packed my bag. I didn't have much, and I took the set of works out of the mattress.

I walked back into the living room and threw the works at Barb's feet.

"It wasn't sex," I said.

She bent down and picked up the works.

"Oh, like this would be better?" she asked, eyebrows stretched across her forehead.

"I'm not a snitch," I said.

"Hope you like prison," she said as I was walking back out the door.

Waiting for me in the dirt parking lot like a trusty steed was my old green Cutlass. I unlocked the door and was about to get in when I heard my name being called. I looked up and saw Randall heading toward me, carrying a small suitcase.

"What are you doing?" I asked.

"Not staying in this fucking place," he said.

"Well, get in," I said.

He got in the passenger side. I cranked the engine and we officially became "splittees."

The Law Won

I intend to keep the description of what happened next short and sweet. This is because it is difficult to admit anyone could be quite as stupid, as willfully self-destructive as Randall and I were in the one week of our freedom.

Once we had free access to each other's bodies, of course, neither of us was particularly interested. I'd had a big crush on him and he'd had one on me, but the circumstances were artificial. We were co-conspirators in the treatment center, but outside we were utterly at a loss. My mother was gone for the summer, so we laid up in her apartment, but we had no money, and I didn't have any drugs to make it possible to live with myself after yet another failure. Barb's utter rejection of me hurt worse than I could admit. "Pack your shit and get out." She knew how to destroy a girl.

Randall and I passed the time in petty crimes of one sort or another. We ate a fine dinner of lobster tails at an expensive restaurant and slipped out without paying the bill. We went to the grocery store and loaded up a grocery cart with food and beer and then trotted right out the side door, grocery cart and all. It was bizarre how we seemed to get away with whatever we tried. But petty crimes weren't going to bail us out of the little boat of self-loathing that was slowly slinking beneath us.

So I suggested the only thing I knew how to do at this point.

"Let's rob a drugstore," I said, as we sunned ourselves on the little patio outside my mom's apartment.

"Are you fucking crazy?" he asked. "With what?"

"We'll pawn the TV, get a gun, and after we rob the drugstore, we can get the TV back," I suggested.

"Are you fucking crazy?" he asked again.

"You can wear a wig," I told him.

"Me? I'm doing this?" he said.

I looked at him and nodded. You may not believe this, but Randall wasn't generally stupid. In fact, he was a pretty bright guy. But not this time. And I'm pretty sure that if I wind up as a homeless, three-legged dog in my next life it will be because I convinced this guy, who was a little unstable but not outright bad by any stretch of the imagination, to agree to this ridiculous plan.

Why did it never occur to either of us to just go get a job? The only reason I can think of is that we somehow felt we needed punishment. We hated ourselves that much.

So we did it. We got a cheap little handgun from the pawnshop. Randall put on a wig — an Afro of all things — and I drove him to a drugstore. A few minutes later he ran out with a bag full of bills. I was parked behind a restaurant next door. He jumped in the car.

"Go, go, go!" he said. So I put the car in drive and drove fast but without breaking the speed limit.

"I was so scared I pulled off the wig," he said, laughing in sheer horror and fear.

"Did you get any drugs?" I asked, the only thing I cared about. This is the part of the story, if you hadn't guessed, where I have hit rock bottom. I have only a sliver of my soul left at this point.

"No, I just got some money."

What good was money, I thought.

We weren't back at my mom's apartment twenty minutes before the cops were pounding on the door. Apparently, a concerned citizen had seen Randall jump in my car and called the cops. She'd had the wits about her to write down my tag number, which we'd been too stupid to obscure. We tried to go out the back door but they were waiting for us there. They must have been amazed to encounter such imbecilic criminals as the two of us.

They took us to separate jails. And that was the end of our week-long crime spree.

Comfortably Numb

A few hours later, I am standing naked in a shower, and a woman in a uniform sprays my arm pits, my head and my pubic hair with some kind of horrible-smelling bug spray, and I crash in a head-on collision with reality.

The jail cell where I stay waiting for my trial is out at the Duval County prison-farm. This is nothing like the Lake City jail. This is like a miniature prison with sliding, clanging doors and women officers who have seen my kind plenty. I am put in a cell that is a kind of dormitory with twelve bunks. The walls of the cell are turquoise. The bars are painted black. The chrome toilets and showers are right out in the open. Anyone can walk by and watch you take a shower or a shit.

I find an empty bunk and lie down. This time I'm not kicking. I wasn't out of the rehab long enough to get a habit. That makes it worse. This time there is no reason for me to be here. I have no excuse.

In the wall there are four narrow windows. They are deep windows with several thick sheets of Plexiglass between the inner wall and the outer wall.

I stare at those slices of sky. They turn from black to light purple to orangish-pink to white. And in the evening they reverse the process. Sometimes the color is dark purple, sometimes it is periwinkle blue. I am astounded, and I cannot remember ever seeing beauty that moved me so. It's the only thing that I feel, and I am grateful for it.

Most of those who come into the cell are short-timers. They've been picked up for drunk and disorderly, hooking, or shoplifting and after a few days they're gone. One older lady, a big woman with blue-black skin, comes in. She sings hymns all the time. At first it gets on my nerves, but then it just becomes part of the scenario, what a friend I have in Jesus. I cannot remember a time when these songs were not constantly being sung.

She's been there about a week when I notice she isn't singing anymore. I look down on the floor. She is convulsing, her eyes have rolled back in her head, and a pool of piss has formed on the floor underneath her. She's having an epileptic fit. I've never seen one before, but I know that's what this is. Other women in the cell scream for the guards. Someone yells, "Get a comb. Stick it in her mouth."

I stay on my bunk, and I watch everything. A white-haired woman with a bunch of keys runs in and then two male guards come in and carry the hymn-singer away. After it's over, I mentally search every part of my being, looking for some sign of feeling. But there is nothing, except a vague irritation with myself that I didn't even care about what happened to that woman. That wise-ass voice in my head says to me, "You are fucked up, babe." But I know that much.

I stayed in the un-sentenced cell about six weeks and made good friends with a chick from D.C. who had gotten busted because she entrusted some coked-up guy to return a rental car for her. The rental car was never seen again. So she was doing time for car theft. She and I played chess every day, and we talked about this revolution we were gonna have. We figured out how to make the world perfect, and we covered it all—education, politics, social policies. She was a damn good chess player.

Every morning half of the cell had to get up and clean the cell. We were in different groups, but on her mornings, she was the only one who'd get up to clean.

"Damn, girl," I told her. "Wake those others up and tell them to help you."

But she didn't do it. She just cleaned the whole cell by herself. The third time that this happened, the C.O. came in and made the others get up and help her clean.

Later that afternoon as I dozed, I heard a nasty tone buzzing around the cell. I woke up and looked over at the three beds lined up against the other wall. In those beds were three women that I'd been getting along O.K. with, but now they were shooting venom my way.

"Look at her, pretending that she's asleep," one of them said.

"What are you talking about?" I asked.

"Oh, like you don't know. Like you haven't heard every word we said," another said.

I hadn't heard them, but I could surmise what the hostility was all about.

"The guard didn't hear me say anything," I shot at them. "All she had to do was look in here herself and see y'all sleeping while Hannah did all your work."

"See, the bitch was awake the whole time," one of them said.

"Fuck this," I said and lay back down. Jail had numbed me up or I would have been more scared. Then again, what could I do about it? These women were pissed off at me, and nothing I could say was going to change their minds. If someone wants to hate you, they will, no matter what you do or say. One of that brood really wanted to hate me. I knew her from the street, and she sold me some shit for dope one time. She knew it and I knew it.

"She thinks she's cute," she sneered.

They leaked poison from the sides of their necks after that but no one touched me.

Finally, the day of my sentencing arrived. I was allowed to wear street clothing. I had to wait in a holding cell for a long time with the other women. Most of them were poor and illiterate. Their faces were expressionless. The bailiff opened the door and called my name. I stood up, straightened out my skirt, and walked into the same courtroom where Charlie had gotten sentenced five years earlier. My attorney was a round little man, very businesslike and smart, an old friend of my mother's. I noticed my mother in the front row.

The judge looked at me, shook his head like he just couldn't believe this. I held my hands behind my back, and though I shoved all my fear back into a dark corner in the farthest recesses of my mind, I still couldn't help twisting my fingers as I waited for him to tell me how long I was going down for. My lawyer has said I could get ten years, which meant I would do probably seven. I'd be almost thirty years old.

I stood before the judge. I knew I had no right to pray, so I didn't. I tried not to think about watching Charlie get sentenced to ten years. I tried not to think about what ten years would be like. I felt as if I were made of plaster. It wouldn't take much to crack me. Maybe Reverend Collins said the prayer that I couldn't because the judge wiped his forehead quickly and said, "Two years in prison, followed by three years' probation."

Thank you, God, I whispered. Thank you. Thank you. Thank you. It was all I could do not to cry.

That day I got moved over to the sentenced cell of the county prison farm while I waited for them to ship me down state. Could be a week, maybe a month, the officer told me. They usually waited until they had two or three prisoners needing to make the trip. Meanwhile I had to work with the other sentenced inmates—the ones doing less than a year and who wouldn't be going down to the joint.

I worked in the kitchen. Which meant I had to get up at about four-thirty every morning. I always had a headache from waking up that early but at least I had something to do with myself which was better than the unmitigated boredom of the un-sentenced cell. We fixed stuff like grits, scrambled eggs, sausage, pancakes with a molasses that tasted like pulverized worms. Then after breakfast we cleaned. I washed monstrous sized pans. Nothing bothered me though. I couldn't feel a fucking thing in jail. Except for the headaches every morning.

My friend Hannah got sentenced to county time so we had a few weeks to hang out together before I was taken down to the state prison. She also worked in the kitchen. One afternoon, a couple of male inmates brought in some fresh vegetables from the farm. The men were hot and sweaty from the work. We flirted with the men. Then one of them said something about how good the vegetables would taste with his sweat on them.

"Good masculine sweat," he said. We glanced at each other and our eyes said, disgusting. We didn't flirt with them anymore. Fresh vegetables were a rarity on the jailhouse menu which mainly featured delicacies such as neckbones and rice. When the sweaty male inmates brought in fresh vegetables, Hannah and I were thrilled.

"Cucumbers," we said in delight, and those dolts leered and thought we were going to fuck the cucumbers. As if sex could possibly be more important than a really good salad.

A week or so later, it was time to transport me to the prison. So I said good-bye to Hannah.

"Are you scared?" she asked.

"Yes," I said. "I am scared."

Into This World

In prison, I am not raped by a gang of women with a toilet plunger, no muscled-up stud with tattoos on her tits claims me for her wife, no one corners me in the laundry room to beat the shit out of me. It's not like the movies. The guards don't sodomize me; the warden doesn't devote his every waking moment to making my life "a living hell." The warden doesn't even know my fucking name.

This particular place also doesn't look anything like the prisons on television or in movies—no honeycomb of cells tier upon tier. Instead, low buildings are spread out across grassy hills. We have six dorms, a chapel, a cafeteria, a factory, a huge laundry facility, an education building and an administration building. Large windows let the morning light pour into the dorms, and because there are just a few low trees, in the early mornings as we trudge to breakfast, we can witness Technicolor sunrises.

But it's still prison with guard towers, double fences and razor wire. It is not a country club; it is a void. The place where nothing happens. You are in the fishbowl but all the fish are swimming outside. And the water level inside the bowl is very low. You gasp for something, but you don't know what.

I have the corner bunk in the dorm that I share with forty other women. There is a green blanket on my bed and I have a metal dresser with two drawers. In the drawers I keep my state pajamas, my state jeans, my free world jeans (we are allowed to have two pairs), my two state work shirts, my two state dresses, my state bathrobe, and my state socks. I keep my state sneakers under the dresser. The state work shirts are big and comfortable. The state jeans are ridiculous—the crotch is somewhere around knee-level.

A soft-spoken black woman lives in the bunk next to mine—our bunks are our homes, our addresses. She keeps pictures of her three children—two girls with bows in their hair and a boy wearing a bow tie—on her dresser. She knits most of the time and is pleasant enough though we don't have all that much to say to each other. She's doing fifteen years. I don't know what for. What I do know is that sometimes she cries for her children and she grinds her teeth at night. The other inmates call her "Mother."

My best friend is a woman named Leigh. She's 25, and she has wispy blond hair. She has wide blue eyes, a ski slope nose, and freckles. She has a laugh that is more infectious than the flu. When I wake up every morning, the first thing I do is look across the dorm to see if she is up yet, to make sure she is still there. She does the same thing.

We get up most mornings when the buzzer goes off at 6:30. If you want to eat breakfast, that's when you get up. If you don't care about breakfast, then you can sleep in for another hour. Work starts at 8, and you better not be late unless you want them to bring out the dogs and start looking for you.

Leigh and I almost always get breakfast. Sometimes it's pancakes, and even though the syrup is something strange with no relationship at all to maple, it is still a breakfast worth going for. Other times breakfast might be powdered eggs and cold grits and toast. On those mornings we eat the toast. We also drink the coffee, which is terrible and tastes nothing like free world coffee, but you get used to it and eventually find that you'll drink it without complaint.

Whatever happens on the compound, Leigh knows about it. Everyone likes and trusts Leigh. This is not an asset. Leigh has already gone to solitary once for helping somebody out. She picked up some pills somebody threw over the fence for one of the other women. No one else would go get them, so Leigh said she would do it. Then she got caught and did thirty days in the box. She says they wouldn't let her smoke or have anything to read except the Bible and that she only got to shower twice a week. I don't have nearly so many friends as Leigh does. I get along okay.

There are three other chicks we hang with—Misty, Jo Ellen, and Tonya. Misty and Jo Ellen have never shot drugs in their lives, and they help keep the rest of us from constantly lapsing into old-days-dope-talk. We all usually sit outside the dorm on the weekends, listening to the radio and trying to get a tan. We have to roll up our shorts and our work shirts, and the black women look at us like we're crazy. They go inside and play cards while we sit out on the beach and torture ourselves with memories of other lives.

It is on these weekend afternoons I realize that what I miss is not my old life at all but a life I never had. I miss going to Key West with a man, drinking margaritas and slipping on rocks in the warm water. I miss going to foreign movies. I miss drinking coffee with friends and talking about politics. I miss shopping for new clothes, going to punk rock concerts. I miss having a nice apartment in a city. I miss parties. During the past six years, I never went to a single party. I didn't buy a single record album. Being a junkie was a job, a 24-seven job.

This other life—the one that I miss—is nebulous to me at first, but I start to keep a list. The first item on the list is Key West. I put margaritas in parenthesis. I have lived in Florida most of my life and never once been to the Keys—too busy getting stoned to have any fun. But I know that the water is as warm as a good narcotic, and it looks like liquid islands of blue and turquoise and green. If I close my eyes, I can hear seagulls.

But there are plenty of other things besides Key West on the list.

My brother got me a subscription to the *Sunday New York Times*, and I get a lot of my ideas from the magazine. I put Visit New York City on the list and "Broadway Plays." I read an article about wedding chapels in Lake Tahoe and I put "get married at Lake Tahoe" on the list. Dublin goes on the list. A new blue car. I put college on the list, too. Then just for kicks, I write, "Magna Cum Laude."

In one of the magazines, I read an article about cave divers and how they use a rope to guide themselves out of the lightless blue-black caves. I think about what that must be like—swimming blind like that and if you let go of the rope, if you drop your flashlight, you're lost forever. It all feels familiar.

Leigh and I cut out pictures of the pretty men from the Sunday New York Times Magazine and tape them to the inside of our lockers. "A Man Who is Not a Junkie" goes on the list. When I lie in my bed at night and look at my list, I run my finger over this last item and wonder if there is someone out there who could love me—someone who is not a junkie. The question wounds me. I'm glad I have a corner bunk next to the wall, so I can turn my face away.

Mother stays on her bunk most of the time with two big skeins of yarn on the smooth blanket below her. I can hear the click-clicking of those plastic needles. Steel needles, of course, are not allowed.

"You, O.K., Bunkie?" she asks every once in a while without looking up from her yarn.

"Fine," I always answer, for how can someone with only two years dare to complain to a woman doing fifteen?

We never say we are in prison. Rather unimaginatively, we say we are in hell. I remember reading "No Exit" when I was about fifteen, and this place is a pretty accurate rendition. We are all trapped with people we really don't want to be with—for eternity, it seems.

Things I hate about prison: the noise, the unrelenting shouting, yelling, loud discussions, conversations maintained at full volume, never getting to go to the bathroom or take a shower behind a closed door, the fact that after every visit from my mom a correctional officer looks up each of my orifices, the noise that goes on even after every one is asleep (the farts, coughs, grunts and teeth grinding), the fact that we never get fresh fruit or vegetables, the gnats that have to be waved away from our dinner trays during summer, the noise in the cafeteria.

All that noise never manages to silence this little voice in my head, words coated in sarcasm, that says thing like, "This was a great idea. Hey, let's rob a drugstore. Why have a normal life when you can come to this vacation paradise?" Then the voice does a trombone slide into utter contempt and adds, "You stupid bitch."

No one in prison is innocent.

We are in here for strangling our babies, running over our husbands, forging checks, B&E, robbing drugstores, robbing liquor stores, holding up convenience stores. We are in here for possession of a gram of cocaine, a ton of marijuana, stolen property. We are in here for kicking an old man to death for three dollars. We are in here for helping our boyfriend kidnap and rape another woman. We are in here for racketeering, for extortion and embezzlement, for vehicular manslaughter. We are junkies, alcoholics, imbeciles, geniuses, bikers, gang members, hookers, debutantes, abused wives, and unlucky. The youngest of us is fourteen, the oldest is 67.

I become a model prisoner, and I am not sure how that happens. I have certainly never been "model" anything before in my life. But in prison I toe the line like a ballerina. During the day I go to my job in the printing room, and I operate the litho press. After work I volunteer for extra cleaning jobs, I'm always on my bunk for count, I don't fight with anyone, I don't "homosex." I play backgammon, chess or scrabble at night. I tutor other women who want to take their G.E.D. tests. I don't join in when the white women bitch about the black women, and I don't pay attention when the black women bait the white women. I read, stay calm, and keep focused. From all appearances I am ready to take my place in the citizenry.

But at night, my dreams erupt in battle. In them I am running through a tunnel. A man who looks like a wolf chases me. I get in the Cutlass. I'm driving, but my headlights won't work. The darkness closes in on me, getting darker and darker. I'm pushing the accelerator but the car won't move. I stomp on the pedal, and I can see the speedometer edging up towards 120 miles an hour, but the still the car is not moving forward. Instead it is rolling over and over and darkness is ripping the skin off my face. Then I hear Charlie's voice, saying, "It's just you and me, baby."

In another dream, I live in a wooden ice-house in the country with my mother and my brother. We're always trying to get warm because it's so cold in the house, and we set fires on top of huge ice blocks. Suddenly the curtains are on fire. I try to put out the fire, beating it with my bare hands until my brother grabs me and drags me into the yard. I stand in the yard and watch as he rushes back into the now blazing house to get my mother. Through the window I can see both of them burning alive.

One morning I stand in the hallway in front of the full length mirror and lift my bangs. There are gashes in my forehead.

"Oh my God, Trish, what happened?" Leigh asks.

"I gouged myself last night," I said.

Leigh stares at my reflection in the mirror, then shakes her head and walks off.

Sometimes I claw my arms, sometimes my neck. I have no idea what the dreams mean, but they go on—not every single night, but two or three times a week. In the dreams where no one is after me I am always trying to get high on drugs. I have barrels full of cocaine, garbage bags of heroin, gallons of methadone, but I can never get high. No matter how many drugs I take in my dreams, I never feel them.

I go to the prison shrink with Leigh and the others. He likes us. We have group therapy sessions that don't do anyone any good, but they get us off the compound for an hour a week. And we get to be with a cute man. I go to church, but like all church people, these ones are insane, only more so. They moan and holler in the name of Jesus. The preacher tells us there is only one way, and otherwise we are going straight to hell. I try my best to believe, but would God really use an imbecile like this man for a mouthpiece, I keep wondering. I take the college course that is offered once every six months if they can find someone to teach it. Biology is taught by one of the classification officers, who happens to be a creationist. The dreams continue.

Before I went to prison, I thought people in the joint spent all their time lying in cells reading great books. But I don't get to read as much as I want to. I only manage to get through about one book a week. It's difficult in the noisy dorm so I turn on my radio and put in my earplug to shut out the noise and I train my mind not to hear the radio as I read.

I don't read for pleasure or for escape. I am looking for some sort of explanation—an explanation of this place, of my life, of me coming here. So I read *Crime and Punishment* about an intellectual murderer who finds redemption in a Siberian prison. I whisper his name — Raskolnikov — to myself like a mantra. I love the sound of it, the syllables each like a jab of the knife. I think about the creationist biology teacher and his uninspired God who flipped a switch on the world in seven days. Raskolnikov is like anti-venom, something to counteract the poison of stupidity. I want Raskolnikov's God, but I've no idea where to find it.

Next I read a book called *The Tin Drum* and I fantasize about being able to stay three years old, about being able to scream my way out of my own life, and about Nazis in jackboots clomping through the dorm, pointing their guns at me and then firing, bullets buzzing everywhere like bees. I also read *The Heart of Darkness* about a guy on the Congo River in search of someone named Kurtz. When he finally finds Kurtz, the man is crazy and all he can say is "The horror. The horror." When I'm finished with this book, I hold it and stare at the cover as if that will help me understand it. But it's a mystery to me. I place the book on my dresser and notice that Mother has a white Bible on her dresser. She has pink rollers in her hair, and she is steadily knitting what looks like a blue baby blanket. She notices me watching her.

"For my sister's baby," she says. "It's a boy."

"Oh," I answer. I pick up *The Heart of Darkness* and start over from the beginning.

They keep you busy in prison for obvious reasons. We have our work, our church meetings, our A.A. meetings, our N.A. meetings, our classes of one kind or another. But still we manage to get in trouble. We make hooch in the kitchen. We smuggle in pot and sell toothpick thin reefers for two dollars, we fight sometimes, we steal from each other, we hide in the bathroom and brush each other's hair. We're not allowed to brush or braid someone else's hair because it might lead to "homosexing," but everyone, even model prisoners like me, indulges in this illicit pleasure.

One night Leigh sits next to me in the game room. I'm playing chess with Misty, a little biker chick who had her own Harley out on the streets. Misty has got me in check. Her rook is staring down my king like one of those Iranians having a hoedown in the U.S. Embassy.

"So, did you guys hear about that big retarded girl in C-dorm?" Leigh asks, taking a hand-rolled cigarette from Misty's pack of Bugler and lighting it.

"That ugly whore?" Misty asks. Misty calls all women whores and all men bitches.

Leigh nods her head and blows smoke over our heads.

"Damn, Misty, how'd you get so good? You aren't supposed to be able to beat me," I say. Misty is a paradox, affectionate as a puppy dog, and sharp as a straight razor.

"I'm whipping her ass, Leigh," Misty said, laughing. I finally see my way out of humiliation but it's gonna cost me my queen.

"She went down on about twenty women all in a row," Leigh says in a hush-hush whisper. "They just lined up in the bathroom and went in the stall one after the other."

I look up at Leigh. I'm holding one of Misty's plastic white pawns in my hand, and I'm picturing that moose of a girl with her red hair and her big porcine lips. I feel a tingling between my legs, and I don't want to play to the end of the game anymore.

"Lordy," Misty says. "Twenty? Didn't her tongue get tired?"

Misty takes my queen.

"I concede," I say. Misty studies me suspiciously. I've still got plenty of pieces on the board.

"You can't concede," she says.

"Sure, I can. You win," I say.

Misty clucks her teeth and shrugs her shoulders.

"Okay," she says. "Loser has to put up the game." She gets up with a swish of her long dark hair, kisses Leigh on the cheek which is just illegal as hell, but she gets away with it as usual because the C.O.'s have discovered that she'll even hug them if they let her. Then she takes her Bugler pack and strolls out of the room.

I start putting up the pieces. Leigh is still sitting beside me. She grinds out the cigarette though it's only half smoked. I look over at her again, stare into her eyes. She stares back. What I feel is a certain lurching inside, as if I have taken a step and there is nothing below my feet. I look away.

"So, if you were in C-Dorm, do you think you would have let that girl go down on you?" I ask.

"Trish," she says and grimaces. "Hell, no."

We both know it's not the female-on-female aspect of the thing that bothers us. You expect lesbians when you come to prison, and if you were a junkie on the streets, well, you probably put on a show or two with your girlfriend to get some guy's rocks off and earn yourselves some cocaine or whatever. Hell, most of the couples in this place treat each other with more respect than any hetero-relationship I ever saw. This is different.

"It's like a gangbang in a way," I say, "isn't it? Only she didn't realize it."

I fold the cardboard chessboard over and place it in the box. Outside it is dark, and the windowpanes are black squares covered with steel mesh. I'm thinking how it used to feel—a man's arms, his cigarette scent, his warm breath in my ear, his hand in my hair. Not a particular man, just any man.

"Would you?" Leigh asks me.

"No," I answer. And then I tell her what I never would have told anyone else. "But I would have wanted to."

That night when I go to bed, I don't bother to read any more of *Heart of Darkness*. I think about that lurching feeling, about the darkness inside me—as dark as an underwater cave. I wonder about those twenty or so women who sat down and opened their legs for the girl. How did it feel? The warm and gentle tongue obeying them like a dog? Is that the difference between those of us inside and the people outside? We know? We know just exactly what we are capable of, whether we act on it or not?

After I fall asleep I dream that I am in an enormous stone house. I am sitting by a cold, empty fireplace when I hear a noise at the other end of the house. Somehow I know that a killer is loose inside. I look around the room for some place to hide, but there are only a few couches and one chair. Then I am no longer in the room, but on the staircase and the killer has smelled me. He or she or it is coming after me. I run up the stairs, but it is as if the stairs are rotating in a great circle under my feet and I'm not getting anywhere. I can hear the killer getting closer and closer. I try to scream but my lungs have no air in them. I jump from the stairs and find myself in a bedroom. I slam the door shut and pick up a long cane that I find in the room. I hold up the cane, waiting for the killer to come in. The door opens and he enters. At that moment, I start struggling out of the deep sleep. I force myself to open my eyes. It seems to take a century for me to realize where I am. But when I do, I am so grateful. Even prison is better than the place where I have been. Later I find a long scratch across my cheek.

The next day as we sit in the cafeteria, Leigh nudges me and cuts her sly green eyes toward the red-headed girl standing in line with a goofy smile pasted and crooked like a child's drawing on her pimply face.

Misty sneers and says, "She thinks she's the most beloved bitch on the compound now."

Then Misty starts making these slurping noises, and Leigh and I can't help ourselves. We get the giggles so bad we have to leave before we piss on ourselves. For the rest of the day whenever there's a lull in the conversation, the laughter rushes in to fill it like flooding water. It's horrible.

One of the things I signed up for was art class. Two nights a week, I went to the art room. The art teacher didn't like me from the moment she met me—she told Leigh she thought I was a phony, maybe she knew the model prisoner bit was just a facade, maybe she didn't like my smile—but I went anyway. I would take a hunk of clay and throw it into the center of the wheel. Then placing my elbows firmly on the sides, I would hold the spinning clay in my wet hands. My thumbs would press down into the middle of the lump and slowly, slowly I would pull out a bowl or a jar. Something about this action, the clay spinning around and around and the feel of it in my fingers was mesmerizing and even seductive. When I pulled a shape out of the mass, I thought of a midwife pulling a baby from its mother's womb. I made coffee cups for me and Leigh. I made a coffee cup for Mother. She gave me a maroon and white afghan in return.

It is the slow fade of spring into summer. One night I leave the art room to go back to the dorm. A bush by the door of the art room thrusts dozens of voluptuous white gardenias into the air, spreading heady beams of scent in a wide radius. I pull the aroma with me as I walk "home." No one else is with me and it is one of those incredibly rare moments in prison when I am actually alone. I stop at the steps that lead down to my dorm and take a moment to study the night sky. You can never see stars like this in the city. Looking up, I almost forget where I am. For just a second I am standing on a beach in the Florida Keys. And then the oddest thing happens.

All around me it seems as if everything is a projection—the glittering stars, the succulent gardenias, the cockroach on the sidewalk, the dorm with its big lighted windows like blank eyes. I'm part of the projection, too—an elaborate three-dimensional picture always in flux. I think, some day, I'll be in Key West—no, not "some" day. I'll be in Key West right now, because when I get there it will be now. The stars twinkle at me as if I've finally gotten the joke.

Then the door to the dorm opens and the C.O. sticks her head out and says, "Inmate, if you don't want an escape charge, you better get inside here for count."

I go inside the dorm. It is noisy and warm, with women walking back and forth, down the aisles, wearing their slippers and their bathrobes, their faces scrubbed, their mouths all toothpasted, and I feel a strange affection for them and for the sound of their voices intertwining in discordant melodies. I think about the red-haired girl in her dorm, how all of us just want the same thing, and how we're not different. Not really.

I look over at Leigh's bunk. Her head is bent, and I can see that she's writing a letter, probably to her mom or her dad. I don't disturb her, don't call out her name to say good-night. Yes, I am thinking, I do have a dark, dark heart. But even in the darkest part of it, stars still shine.

I turn my back and go to my bunk. I had planned to wear socks on my hands that night so that I wouldn't scratch myself if I got into one of my nocturnal brawls. But I decide not to. I figure, what the hell, at least I'm doing something in my dreams. Maybe these are the battle I need to have. I close my eyes and before I fall asleep, I think of warm green water and I imagine the taste of salt on my lips. Then I step once again into the dark arena.

Been on a Train

The prison was right next to a railroad line. We could look down from the back porch of the dorm and see the tracks on the other side of the razor-wired double fences. If I was out there hanging up my laundry and a train went by, I would stop what I was doing and wait for it to pass. Everything stops when a train is going by. It's a way of letting you know that you're going nowhere, your life is stagnant. The mournful pitch of the train whistle says, so long, so long. How I wished I was on one of those trains, going anywhere.

By and By

Charlotte was doing time for murdering a girl. Her boyfriend was the actual murderer, but Charlotte had been there when he did it. She had helped him take the girl out into the woods. After he killed the girl, they--or he--threw her body into one of the canals in South Florida. The boyfriend then managed to die. He was killed by someone or killed himself, and he left Charlotte holding the bag.

"They thought I was the 'canal killer'," Charlotte told me. "In jail all the other women were threatening to cut me up."

"Who was the canal killer?" I asked. Charlotte had just been transferred up from the maximum-security prison down south. She'd already done five years, and they finally lowered her custody. Now, she was up here where she'd get some job training and supposedly better health care. They said she complained too much at the other place especially after she threatened to file suit when a prison doctor told her she should get pregnant if she wanted to cure her circulation problems.

Charlotte and I both worked in the print shop, and we were on break, sitting outside in the sun.

"He was going around strangling women, hookers and whatnot, and leaving their bodies in the canals," she said. Charlotte had a narrow face, straight brown hair, bad teeth and a cross tattooed between her breasts like a pendant. She never swore, she didn't smoke and she didn't homosex.

“I did some heavy shit before I got busted,” she said.

“You shot dope?” I asked her. She didn’t seem like a junkie to me.

“Yeah, I shot junk,” she said. I nodded. There was a difference between someone who shot junk and someone who was a junkie. Not like being one was any better than the other, just different.

She didn't talk much about her crime, and when she did, it was always in this sort of hushed voice, her eyes searching the sky, as if even now that boyfriend might be waiting for her. All I got out of her was that this guy had a powerful hold on her--a power he “bargained with the devil” to get.

“There wasn’t nothing I wouldn’t do if he told me to do it,” she would say and shake her head as if she still couldn’t believe it.

In prison Charlotte went to church every Sunday, vespers every Wednesday and Bible study whenever she could. She wanted me to come to Bible study with her, but I wouldn't.

I came walking into the print shop one morning and Charlotte wasn’t there.

“Hey, boss man,” I said to the dude who ran the program. “Where’s Charlotte?”

“She won’t be coming in this week,” he said. “She’s gone to Circle for the week.”

“Circle?” I said. “Shit.”

“Watch your language, young lady,” the boss said, and I just laughed because he didn’t care as long as we did the work that was contracted—mostly just running off stuff for the prison system, newsletters for the prison staff and that kind of thing. In fact, he had a crush on me, and I used it to get free world candy and the occasional blunt which I would sell.

My days were like that, every day the same thing. It was like taking a battleship across the Pacific Ocean—every day the same monotonous blue waves, the same limitless dome above. Get up, eat breakfast, go to work, eat lunch, go to the dorm for count, go back to work, eat dinner, spend a half hour out on the softball field, go back to the dorm, read or maybe go to the art room or the chapel, then in bed by ten. Of course, we created storms—little dramas—for we were all women who had thrived on drama in our outside lives. We had loved the violent explosions with our men, the adrenaline surge at the sight of a cop car, the angry confrontations with people who got in our way, people who wanted to shoot us or were going to be shot by us. We had thought we hated it, but prison showed us what we really hated—sameness, the quotidian, lives empty of excitement. Sometimes I felt the wildness in me twirling around, ready to spin out of the top of my head, but I stuffed it back down. Because I couldn't spend another minute longer than I had to in prison.

"Why did she have to go to the Circle?" I asked one of the other print shop workers who was sitting at the table with me as I collated pieces of paper together and stapled them. Circle was one of those "feel good" therapeutic programs some joker thought would rehabilitate us.

"'Cause it looks good on your paper, fool," she answered.

"Hey, I'll go to church and I'll volunteer to clean every stinking toilet in this joint, but I am not going to Circle for anybody," I said. "I don't care how good it looks on paper."

I worked all week without Charlotte to talk to except if she came and sat with us at lunch, which was rare. She didn't talk much when I was with my buddies—Leigh, Tonya, Misty and the rest of them. We were all still bad girls in our hearts and Charlotte wasn't.

Next Monday morning Charlotte was back in the print shop. I had missed her and her crooked toothed-smile. She had this quiet, wise demeanor, this way she'd look at you out of the corner of her eyes before bursting into laughter. During break we went over to the canteen and each bought a Mickey Mouse ice cream bar. We sat on the grass outside the building and ate. I bit off each ear and then devoured the rest.

"You're getting chubby, professor," Charlotte said. She was all skin and long sharp bones.

"I know. It's how I deal with sexual frustration," I said. "What do you do?"

"Church," she said. "And now the Circle."

"What?" I said, the ice cream starting to taste sour in my mouth as I rolled that word "circle" around the insides of my skull.

"Trish, the Circle is real good. They asked me if I want to be a Circle leader," she said. "You oughta try it."

"No," I said. "I had enough circles in those fucking drug programs. I am not going to some circle."

"It's not like that," she said. "It's only inmates in there. No guards. Just this one lady who comes in sometimes, but she doesn't even work for the state. I can't hardly believe they have it on the compound. It's like some great big secret."

"Yeah, well they had junkies running those drug programs and I saw how great that was," I answered. But Charlotte gave me a deep look that she'd probably learned from her killer-boyfriend.

"This ain't no drug program," she said evenly.

Just then the Boss man came out and said, "I hate to disturb you ladies, but you better get the hell in here and start printing off these orders or I'll fire both your asses."

"Fire us?" I said.

"Would you rather work in the laundry, Inmate?" he asked.

"No," I answered, getting up and following him in a hurry. I sure as hell did not want to work in the laundry.

I didn't want to talk to Charlotte after that, but she sat beside me after I'd run off about 500 instructions for weapons discharge regulations on the old noisy printer.

"They've got coffee in there—free world coffee," she said.

"I don't care. I've got a jar of Taster's Choice in my locker right now," I answered and juggled a stack of paper in my hands.

"I don't mean instant," she said. "I mean brewed. Maxwell House. All you can drink."

Brewed Maxwell House. I was back home, sailing across the Hart Bridge with the smell of the coffee plant licking the back of my throat.

"And popcorn, too," she said. "With butter." The butter clinched it.

"All right," I said. "All right. I'll sign up for a goddamn circle." After all, it only lasted a week.

Two weeks later Charlotte no longer worked in the print shop. She had been asked to work in the Circle as a leader. Circle leaders were an elite group in a way that was difficult to define. There were only five of them on the whole compound. Circle leaders did not homosex, were never supposed to get written up for anything, and occasionally got to leave the compound. They never cursed and didn't get in fights. The funny thing is that no one really hated them. In fact, most people liked them. I watched Charlotte and her new friends and decided that they were an anomaly—like the Hawaiian Islands that bloom out in the middle of the Pacific Ocean.

On a Monday morning I walked into the trailer where the Circle groups were held. I sat down in a circle of metal chairs with eleven other inmates. Then one of the leaders sat in the circle with us and told us this story about "warm fuzzies and cold pricklies." It was about a town full or people who gave each other warm fuzzies, but then someone told them they'd run out of warm fuzzies and so they started giving away cold pricklies instead.

I listened to the story and tried not to roll my eyes at its predictability, its simple-mindedness, the lack of complexity, the sentimentality, the obviousness of the message. But when one of the leaders came behind me and began to rub my shoulders in a most soothing manner and explained that this was a "warm fuzzy," I thought perhaps the story wasn't so bad, after all.

A little later, the leaders fixed coffee for us.

"You want some cream or sugar?" one of them asked me.

I looked at the woman next to me. She looked at me. No one in prison ever asked you if you wanted something. I'd gotten used to not having cream or sugar in my coffee because if you had any in the dorm, people would come mooch it off you.

"I'll take a little bit of both," I said.

Over the course of the week, we did different exercises. In one of them we had to get in groups of four and start our own business.

Some of the businesses were cottage industries like sewing or baking—that kind of thing.

"Shit, I can't do anything," I said to my group. I'd gotten in with the dope fiend group. We didn't have any skills among the five of us except boosting, forging and lying on our backs.

"Well, what did you get busted for?" one of them asked me.

"Driving the car for a robbery," I said.

"I can drive a car like Mario Spaghettio," someone else in the group said.

And so we decided to start a limousine service. We designed some sexy little uniforms and came up with a name for the business and figured out how we'd get a loan to start off with. When I walked out of the trailer that afternoon, I was laughing with this tough old hen that had always scared me with her yellowy eyes. And I was embarrassed to have been won so easily.

When one of the Circle leaders, a woman named Jill, got paroled a month later, Charlotte came up to me after dinner and told me that the other leaders had decided to ask me to join them. We stood outside the cafeteria while gangs of women walked past on their way to spend their half-hour of free time in various manifestations of doing nothing.

"I don't know," I said. "I like the print shop."

Charlotte didn't say anything. She just waited.

I could see the highway far down the hill on the other side of the fences and the woods. I thought about that week and how it seemed as if I wasn't even in prison whenever I was in that trailer. I had said yes to a lot of things in my life, and most of them were mistakes. Why stop now, I said to myself.

"Yeah," I said. "Yeah, I'll do it."

Morning Has Broken

"Be a soprano," the choir director said. "We need somebody in the front row." So I stood between Misty and Dee, a woman I'd bought heroin from a few times in the old days.

I joined the choir not because I suddenly got all religious, but because I wanted to sing again. My mother had been a choir director and voice coach. She'd tried to teach me to sing. She said I had a good voice, but I knew better. I couldn't carry a tune in a bucket. And yet the fact that I wasn't much of a singer never stopped me from enjoying it.

In the prison choir, we sang, we shouted, we clapped. We let the Lord come down on us. It was all good fun and silliness—the one place prison wasn't like prison, well, two places if you counted the Circle. Prison still wasn't a good place to be. But If I could learn to like a few things in prison, I could learn to like a lot of things on the outside.

At drug program number two, Barb had said I had no *joie de vivre*. She said I would go queer if I ever went to prison because all my problems stemmed from some twisted need I had, that I couldn't live without someone in my thrall. She called me a femme fatale. I was afraid that she was right, and I knew this was my only chance. Because her words flashed in my mind every time some stud looked at me, I didn't hook up in prison. I looked for other things to do with my time. So I sang in the choir, and when the visiting prison ministry types came to see us, we sang for them.

One day a woman from the outside, one of those smiling church types, came up to me after the service and said, "God has a plan for you." That's a standard line for those people. They probably even believe it.

"I mean it," she said. "I looked at your face and I just felt it."

I smiled at her and then looked for a way to get away as soon as I could. I mean, what do you say when someone says that to you?

And then it happens. I had thought I was going to escape the standard cliché of prison life, the moment of truth and healing, the awesome Hand of God.

But one Sunday morning—Easter morning to be exact—one Sunday morning the choir gets to go outside to a free world church. The preacher is a black man in whose mouth the name of Jesus is a blossoming flower. Our choir sings for them, "Morning has Broken." And their choir sings gospel for us.

The end of the service comes, and the preacher has us all get in a giant circle. I wind up holding the hand of a tall copper-skinned man. His gorgeous young wife stands on the other side. At first I think the giddiness comes from holding the firm hand of an actual man. But then in a second, I forget the man is even there.

That Sunday morning something rises up inside me, and it is bigger and deeper and wider and more powerful than an atom bomb. The earth falls out from underneath my feet. I'm not sure what I'm feeling because I've never thought of God in this way, and it doesn't feel like a person or like anything I've ever imagined, except I know it's what I was trying to get to every time I stuck a needle in my arm. It rises up and opens every door in my heart and my head. Something cool as a rainbow flows in.

For three days I walk around in a daze. For three days I am not even in prison. I am walking in another dimension. Leigh asks me what is going on, and I try to explain it to her. It's like doing the best heroin and the best cocaine in one shot, I tell her. Only better because you don't grind your teeth.

When it finally wears off, I don't know what to think. I wonder what I could have done to hold on to it. I'm not sure if I've changed, but I'll never be able to deny what happened to me. I can never again pretend that there isn't something beyond all this.

My mother comes to visit me. As I look at her, at the soft way her eyes go out of focus sometimes, I remember the overwhelming love I'd felt for when I was a child. I'd wanted to defend her, to hurt the people who hurt her. At the time I didn't realize the enormous reserves of strength she had. And I would not fully understand those reserves until many years later when she would battle the vicissitudes of old age the way she had once gone to battle for me.

On this day, my mother looks resolute and pulls a piece of paper out of her purse.

"Sign this," she says and hands me an application form for the university.

"I called the Department of Corrections," she says. "You should be out in time for the spring semester."

Right now I can't imagine ever leaving. Then I remember the college girls in the coffee shop that I used to see when I went there with Barb. Hell, I've done college before. I was awful at it, but maybe I'd be better this time.

"I think I'll major in philosophy," I tell my mother as I sign the paper.

"When you find out the meaning of life, tell me what it is," she says.

I tap the end of the pen on the round table where we are sitting.

"Nah, not philosophy. Literature. Can you major in literature? You know, just sit around reading books all day?" I ask her.

"Sure, you can major in it, and then you can sell encyclopedias when you graduate," she says.

"Beats robbing drug stores," I say to her.

She tilts her head and gazes at me. There is something about the look that passes between a mother and a daughter, something in it that reaches all the way back to the moment when you were at her breast.

Her hazel eyes are full of sonatas. Somehow I have to make it through the summer and then through work release without screwing up. The God feeling is gone, and there's a long dark tunnel ahead of me.

This Bird Has Flown

And so it came. Three days and a wake up. Two days and wake up. One day and wake up. Then the wake up. I'd been accepted into the work release program and that was the day I would transfer. I went to the cafeteria and ate breakfast with Leigh. She didn't say much. We both wondered if we'd ever see each other again.

We went back to the dorm. Some people clapped me on the back, told me to take care, others just walked on by as if I wasn't there. It was a weird feeling—good, but I felt guilty for my happiness. And Leigh, sweet Leigh. She didn't seem to want to leave my side.

"You be careful, girlfriend," she said as I emptied out my locker.

"I will," I said.

"And get laid for me, okay?"

"Sure."

The brown dress stepped out of her office, looked at Leigh, and said, "Inmate, haven't you gone to your work assignment yet?"

"I'm going right now," Leigh said. Then she hugged me with the brown dress standing right there, and she quickly shoved a card into my hand. I watched her walk out of the dorm, wearing her black and white saddle oxfords, and I remembered the first time I saw her, wearing red-framed sunglasses. One of the other inmates had said, "That Leigh is a cool white girl." That was no lie.

I got on the white bus with screens on the windows to go to Gainesville about an hour later. As I was boarding, someone yelled, "Don't look back, Trish." I thought it might have been Leigh's voice, but I couldn't be sure because I damn sure wasn't looking back. That's the surest way to come back they all said.

When I sat down, I opened the card she had given me. Inside she'd drawn a picture of two little girls in pigtails and overalls. Yeah, I thought, all right, wipe out the past, start fresh and innocent. As the bus rumbled over the pavement, I felt myself going away.

Trees hung over the road as we passed through rural Florida. We went by pine farms—the thin trees like pencils in perfect rows—and we went by fields of bright green alfalfa grass. My eyes ate up the landscape.

I was as scared as I had been going to prison. I tried to tally up the changes, but really you couldn't know if any of those changes were real until you got out there and test drove your new self. What was different, I wondered? I didn't feel a need to get high, not yet anyway. I wanted a life, that's what I wanted, but I couldn't picture it, couldn't imagine it. Slow down, I told myself, but my fingers were twisting around each other and my heart started beating fast.

Then we got closer to Gainesville, and along the road the crepe myrtles were blooming—light pink and bright pink and white and purple. They waved in the wind, and I felt as if they were waving me in, waving me into something brand new.

Lots of Laughs, Lots of Laughs

In work release I shared the downstairs bedroom with a sleepy-eyed woman called Tiger. I quickly got a reputation as a goody-goody or a phony, depending on who you talked to. I was trying to put into practice the principles I had learned in the Circle in prison: be warm, be friendly, have a good attitude about life and about yourself. Sure, it wasn't the real me, but the real me had landed me in the joint, and I was trying to find another me who fit. So I was called a phony because I smiled at people and tried to be friendly. The only person this worked with was a gentle and funny Seminole gal, who had just done about a zillion years for murdering someone when she was still a kid. She got released from the prison down south a few days after I arrived, and so I was left pretty much friendless.

I'd had no idea that prison was actually not such a bad place until I got to the work release center. The counselors got all up in your business. I'm not sure what about me rubbed their fur wrong. I guess I didn't bow and scrape enough or maybe my English was too proper for their liking. They needed us to be lower than they were, and I couldn't make myself do the soft shoe shuffle for anyone.

"You're trouble," they told me. They piled on the chores and made sure I missed the bus to my job as a restaurant hostess. They were even rude to my mother when she visited and somehow misplaced the bag of clothes she brought me.

The woman in charge had a degree in psychology, and she decided I was manic-depressive. I couldn't vouch for the manic part, but she was sure digging a deep depressive trench for me to fall into.

There I was, trying desperately to amputate that old junkie self off me because I knew the way it worked. It lay there waiting like a virus. All it needed was one weak moment. Just one weak moment. Shit. There were a lot of things I wanted to do. I wanted to go to college. I wanted to make good grades and go to football games. I wanted to meet a nice guy. I wanted to get kissed, fondled and fucked insensible. And I wanted to hear someone say that he loved me. I wanted dinner in a fine restaurant. I wanted white wine. I wanted to hold someone's hand and sit by a lake.

But what the other part of me wanted is what I got.

Tiger sat on her bunk, watching me. I felt her eyes on me. Hell, we'd been roommates for two weeks and she hadn't said one damn word to me so far.

"So you shot up before you went to prison?" she asked.

I looked over at her, the ghost-gray eyes, the thick brown-blond hair, her upper lip hooked as if she were only asking the most casual questions. I'd been reading this great story in the Bible about Paul getting bit by a viper and just shaking that sucker right off his hand.

"I was a junkie for six years," I said. I went back to reading. The Bible isn't exactly light reading.

"I never shot up," she said wistfully.

I looked back over at her. I was lonely. I missed Leigh so badly I could hardly keep from crying half the time. And I was ashamed to miss prison, to miss my friends there. But I did.

"So can you shoot cocaine?" Tiger asked. "I mean I heard you could. I heard it was better than snorting it."

I rearranged the pillow underneath me. Snorting cocaine. My nasal passages burned just thinking about it.

"Sure," I said. "It's the best motherfucking high in the world—for about five minutes, anyway." And I knew that if I had a weakness it was not for heroin or even for Dilaudid, but for that avalanche of rapture that accompanied a shot of cocaine. My toes curled and my stomach roiled just thinking about it.

Tiger was silent for a few minutes. I tried to keep reading, tried to ignore her, but even her breathing was loud.

"You know, one of these girls that was here was a diabetic. She left some of her needles in the bathroom."

My hands released the book.

"You're shitting me," I said. I couldn't believe these Gestapo counselors were such a slack bunch. But, of course, that's why they had to be such vicious wolverines. They were lousy at their jobs, and they must have known it deep down inside. Or maybe they wanted us to screw up.

Tiger came over and sat down on the foot of my bed. She had a warmth about her, an easy smile. She was the kind of person it was impossible not to like if she wanted you to like her.

"I can get some cocaine," she said. "From work."

I stared at her. I felt the room getting watery around me. I didn't want to fuck up my life. I didn't want to go back to prison. But I knew without knowing that I was already falling.

The first time I got her off, I didn't do any myself. That was probably the most astonishing thing I've ever done in my life. But the second time a few weeks later my will had gone the way of my unhappy heart. The counselors were on me from the moment they'd wake me at five in the morning to wash the kitchen floors until I went to bed. For Christmas they gave everyone a little present. Tiger got a bottle of cheap perfume. I got a dog collar. They rode me, sneered at me, and tried to catch me doing anything wrong. So what the hell. I was willing to fuck up like a someone with nothing much to lose even though, in reality, I could lose everything. What they didn't realize was that I had an ally in Tiger.

It is New Year's Eve. We are both due for release but because it is a holiday, they will not release us on January 1. We have to wait a day. Which makes what happens next even more absurd, stupid, and self-destructive than anything I've ever done before. As if I need to make one more leap into the abyss. Like a gambler who can't walk out of the casino with a dollar left to lose.

Tiger has brought home a gram of coke from the sandwich shop. By silent agreement, we get up just after the new year has arrived and we go into the bathroom together. I dump the cocaine into a spoon and squirt water onto it. It dissolves instantly—pure stuff. The chemical smell hits my nose like a ripe rose.

"If this doesn't kill us, death doesn't want us," I say, drawing up our shots into two separate needles. I have stolen that line from one of the religious books that you will find in any institution. Confessionals about how they were bad once, and then God saved them.

Tiger sits on the toilet and ties her arm off with an old piece of pantyhose. She's got prime veins, and I go in right under the bruise that she's developed. I push the cocaine into her system and watch her eyes get swirly as Ferris wheels.

"Get a bell ringer?" I ask. I don't wait for her to answer. I pick up my needle and slide it into my arm. But the coke is only half way in when I fall to my knees and the words "oh no" start running a relay race through my brain. Oh no oh no oh no oh no oh no. This is way too much. Shit. Everything gets frazzled, my heart's clocking 140, and my tongue twists itself into a knot. Fucking terror. I yank the needle out of my arm and shoot the rest of the cocaine into the shower drain. I look over at Tiger and she's gone, baby. She's flying up and away on the wings of death. My brain is an explosion of atoms but after a few wild gasps, somehow I get myself together.

It occurs to me that I could haul ass right now. I could leave her here. I could crawl out one of the bedroom windows and I could run all the way to Alaska. I open the door to leave, but something stops me — maybe it's the ghost of overdoses past.

Instead of leaving, I close the door and take a look at Tiger shaking like an earthquake has hit, and I leap into the routine. The cold water on the chest. The quick slaps on the face, the mouth to mouth. These things help, but what really works are the words. Cocaine is not like heroin. Heroin drowns your will to live, but with cocaine, you just forget how to stay alive. So I use my words. I tell her, come on baby you can do this it's all right we're gonna be fine we're OK come back to me Tiger come on honey it's all right breathe for me OK that's right yes and another breath Tiger breathe take a deep breath.

I keep talking to her in a soft urgent whisper, and in the meantime I'm washing off the spoon. I have to get her off the toilet so I can flush the little plasticine baggie and pieces of needle. Getting her to stand up is nearly impossible. She keeps sinking back down and she's babbling all the while—talking to all these people she sees standing in the little bathroom with us. I press a cold wash cloth to her chest. Then I hold her. I just hold onto her and I pray. A vaporous chill passes over me, a shadow, like someone standing right in the room with us. I close my eyes, and start whispering the only prayer I know by heart: "Our Father, who art in Heaven. . . ."

"Okay," she says after some of the longest minutes of my life.

"Okay what?" I ask. I'm whispering 'cause I know any minute one of the S.S. is going to walk in on us and I'll be wearing pink dresses again.

"Okay," she says again. I pull her up long enough to get the toilet lid up. She sits back down. I push the needles and the baggie between her legs into the water below and I flush.

"Come on, Tiger," I tell her. She nods at me. I get her up again. I open the door to the bedroom. No one else is in the strangely wiggling room. I shut off the bathroom light and lead Tiger to her bed. She lies down.

"Are you all right?" I ask her.

"Yes," she says.

"What's your name?" I ask.

"Tiger."

"Good. I'm gonna be right here all night, Tiger." I tell her. Then I hold her hand and wait for morning.

On January second both of us will walk out of the front door as free women. I will have done my time. I look down at Tiger as she sleeps. She looks like a child, the eyelashes soft against her face, her light brown eyebrows, her skin pale as the morning dawn. I can't do this anymore. I can't go around almost killing people.

"I'm sorry," I whisper. She doesn't hear me, but I've said it and someone in the silence seems to be listening.

Staying Alive

On January second, 1981, I walk out of the doors of the work release center. My mother is there, waiting for me in her Buick. She's going to take me to the place where I'll be living, but first we take a trip to the beach.

It's winter, but the sun is bright and there's no wind so we take off our shoes and walk along the shoreline. I can't help but think of the hell I have put her through, the way she internalizes the pain, but I also feel comforted in her presence. I'm 25 years old and she's in her early 60s, and it feels like we've known each other for lifetimes.

As we walk past the rolling waves of the Atlantic, I wonder: what was the point of all those lost years. Those lost lives? The wasted money? It's not like the junkies I had known all had terrible, deprived childhoods. We weren't manchildren in the promised land. No one beat us with coat hangers or locked us in closets or tortured us in the infinite number of sick ways that some people manage to devise. Sure, some of us were missing fathers or mothers. Some of us had fielded a trauma or two. But others had come from nice little nuclear families in the suburbs. If it wasn't our families, was it something in the culture? I wasn't trying to excuse us, but I wanted to understand the "damage done" and why we wanted to be setting suns, as Neil Young sang.

Maybe we were simply the naked expression of a culture that thrives on addiction--to whiskey and cigarettes, to donuts and coffee, to cars and pretty clothes, to sex, to guns, even to our punitive religions. The questions swirled around my head. It had always seemed that I'd been born without some kind of protective armor that other people had. But maybe that was true of all of us who engaged in these self-inflicted battles. Maybe we were mirrors for other people, and that's why they locked us up.

Traps abound for people like me, and I would need to stay sharp for the rest of my life or they would ensnare me. It would be food, or sex, or drink, or violence. Something would always offer itself as a way to ease the screaming despair inside.

In that moment on the beach with my mom, I understand that I have to accept the despair and figure out how to live with it, or possibly transform it into something else. I've signed up to take a creative writing class at the college. Maybe that's where I'll find the key that unlocks the mystery of what to do with all this shit inside me.

Afterwards, we stop at a seafood restaurant, and I savor every bit of that free-world food — fried shrimp, cole slaw and hushpuppies. Then Mom drives me to the trailer where I've rented a room from Charlotte's sister. Mom hugs me and then drives away. It will be a long time before she trusts that I'm okay, before she can answer my phone calls without trepidation in her voice.

I go inside to unpack my clothes.

The next day I head over to the campus to make a go at a new life. What I don't know is that something inside me is conspiring to make it happen, that friends and lovers are waiting, and teachers are preparing their lessons.

Epilogue

Many readers have asked what happened after the events described in this book. The detailed answer to that question can be found in my follow-up memoir, *My Mother's Requiem*, which is about taking care of my mother in her old age but also about the things that happened in between. You can read the first chapter in the next section, or order it from Amazon at: amazon.com/My-Mothers-Requiem-Daughters-Memoir-ebook/dp/B0CH9CJTN2

The short version is this: after getting my Bachelor's degree at the University of Florida, I worked in various capacities in film, video, and journalism. Eventually I went back to college and got a Master's degree in creative writing from Florida State University and had my first short story published. Later I went back to FSU for a Ph.D. in English and wrote my first novel. Education and writing saved me, which is probably why I ultimately became a writing professor.

I married and had one child. My husband, a video engineer, and I stayed together until our daughter went off to college. In spite of some serious incompatibilities, we had a strong bond, and we raised a terrific child, who grew up to become an advocate for formerly incarcerated people like myself.

Now I'm married to Joe Straub, whom I have known since my college years at the University of Florida, where we both studied with the late, great Harry Crews. Joe is my partner in everything, and without him many of my books would not be published. I am grateful beyond words. You can read more about our relationship on my blog at trishmacenulty.com/2023/02/20/at-long-last-love/.

I am available for speaking engagements, book clubs, and writing workshops. Please contact me through my website trishmacenulty.com if you are interested.

My Mother's Requiem

CHAPTER ONE
SEPTEMBER *2009*

My cell phone starts singing "Love Me Do" at seven in the morning. I've been awake for an hour, lying in bed, thinking, wondering what to do about my crumbling house and my crumbled marriage – abandoned like an old broken sofa by the side of the road. The sound of the phone so early brings on a rush of adrenaline. What now? It's my daughter, Emmy, in a quandary about a paper that's due in an hour. I'm almost grateful to be given a problem that I can handle so easily. I get up and shoot her some suggestions by email. Emmy is in college now and rarely needs my help anymore, but her moment of desperation brings me back to all those times when she was younger and she forgot her homework or lost her keys or had some other mishap and I always ran to the rescue.

A couple of hours later, my friend Darryl calls. He's agreed to go play Scrabble with my mother on Tuesday and Thursday evenings since I have late classes to teach. He wants to know if I've seen my mother this morning. I haven't.

"Well, she wasn't doing well at all last night," he says. "She was very slow and only able to come up with three-letter words. Then when it was time to go, I asked her if she wanted me to take her upstairs. She said no and then she said yes. So I started to walk with her to the elevator. She was wheeling herself, and she turned and went in the other direction. I tried to correct her, but she insisted I was wrong and when I tried to push her wheelchair to the elevator, she began to fight me."

Oh God, I'm thinking, picturing my tiny mother, her mouth set in grim determination, her silver head lowered like a bull, and her hands with their purple bruises clutching the wheels of her wheelchair. And poor hapless Darryl, ever the gentleman, trying to convince her to go the right way.

"I finally let her go in the other direction and then after she couldn't find the elevator, I pushed her the right way but by then she was very upset." And this too, I can imagine: the resigned despair in her eyes, the fluttering hands, the hang-dog look and the inarticulate stammering.

"Yes," I say. "Every time she goes to the hospital she comes back a step lower. I've no idea what to do."

And it's true. I've no idea what to do. They surely won't keep her at The Sanctuary indefinitely if she's that diminished. They do have a memory care unit – a locked door at the end of the hallway. I've never been inside, but I've heard sounds, people calling out, people laughing sometimes, or crying.

It reminds me of a story by Ursula K. Le Guin that I often assign to my students called "The Ones Who Walk Away from Omelas." Le Guin describes a happy, almost perfect society – except for the neglected child kept chained in a basement. This is the price that has to be paid in order for the society to be as delightful and orderly as it is. Everybody studiously ignores the horrid basement and the unspeakable cruelty in which they are all complicit. Though I know the memory care unit is not a bad place nor run by bad people, still, I have ignored it with the same suppressed horror as the people in Le Guin's story ignore the child in the basement.

But why am I even thinking about the memory care unit? We can't afford that. She'd most likely have to go to one of the nursing homes where the lumps of flesh are gathered in their wheelchairs, dozing and drooling and occasionally looking up to ask where they are and if you will take them home.

Then I pause and wonder: maybe it's the new prescription the doctor in the hospital gave her. So I call her family doctor and ask him to "d.c." – discontinue – that medication. Maybe I can buy her a few more months. If she can just make it till February 21 when I plan to take her back to the church in Jacksonville, Florida to hear her music one more time. Her requiem.

About the Author

A former fulltime university professor, Trish lives in Tallahassee, Florida, with her husband. She writes historical fiction, reviews, and feature articles. She also occasionally teaches in the Florida A & M University College of Journalism. For more information and to subscribe to her newsletter, visit her website: trishmacenulty.com

www.ingramcontent.com/pod-product-compliance
Lightning Source LLC
Chambersburg PA
CBHW011236120626
46549CB00009B/3279

* 9 7 9 8 9 8 7 6 4 5 0 5 5 *